# The Northwest Adventure Guide

Pacific Search Press

Pacific Search Press, 222 Dexter Avenue North,
    Seattle, Washington 98109
© 1981 by Pacific Search Press
Printed in the United States of America

Written and compiled by Terri Schell, Christian Kallen,
    Kristen Tregillus, and Craig Sternagel
Designed by Judy Petry

Cover photo: Balloon Excelsior, Inc.

Library of Congress Cataloging in Publication Data

Pacific Search Press.
    The Northwest adventure guide.

    1.  Outdoor recreation—Northwestern States.
I.  Schell, Terri. II. Kallen, Christian. III. Title.
GV191.42.N75P33   1981            917.9            80-24309
ISBN 0-914718-54-1

Wherever you go and whatever you do in the outdoors, move at Nature's pace, seeking not to impose yourself but to lose yourself. If you must leave footprints, make them not with blindness but with care and awareness of the delicate balance around you. And if you must take souvenirs, take them not in your pockets but in your mind and spirit. In preservation lies the promise of renewal.

Pacific Search Press

# CONTENTS

# THE NORTHWEST
# ADVENTURE EXPERIENCE

The Pacific Northwest is a region of uncommon diversity, ranging from sophisticated cities to wilderness, from farmlands to ocean beaches. Here are isolated alpine lakes set amidst mountains two miles high; rivers rich in salmon and trout; forests with rainfall totaling over eighteen feet a year; and sagebrush desert. Here, too, are the great volcanoes of the Cascades—the dormant peaks of Shasta and Rainier, as well as steaming Baker and the unpredictable St. Helens. The long miles of shoreline—from Monterey, California, to northern British Columbia—display as wide a variety of life-forms and landscapes as can be found anywhere. This exciting region—comprising British Columbia, Washington, Oregon, Idaho, and northern California—is the subject of this book, for in the Northwest's diversity lies the potential for great adventure.

Yet what makes the Northwest unique is not only this natural variety but also the accessibility of it all. People have been enjoying the outdoors here for decades, of course, but today, traveling around the world in search of adventure seems both expensive and unnecessary when so much diversity is available close to home. As a consequence, guided trips have become an increasingly popular way to experience all aspects of the Northwest. Canoeing in a Canadian lake brings you silently upon a herd of elk, foraging among willow seedlings. Backpacking along the Oregon coast enables you to appreciate the emergence and submergence of tidal life-forms. Fishing attunes you to the habits of unseen trout; skiing reveals landscapes much different from those of summer; and bicycling allows leisurely appreciation of places you may have driven through dozens of times without really seeing at all. There are many different Northwests and many different ways of experiencing them. And that is why we have compiled this book.

The trips listed in this guide have been selected to reflect the variety of adventure opportunities available to Northwest residents and visitors. The trips are broken down by activity into chapters, each of which has an introduction describing what you can expect from a typical trip. Following each introduction is a list—broken down by state or province to provide easy reference—of the people to contact for details about their programs. In many cases, only one of an operator's many trips is mentioned, so direct communication with that person is advised.

When you choose a trip, make sure you know what to expect. Don't be impressed by the slickness of a brochure—experience counts much more than financial backing in many cases. Ask the operator about his or her own experience, and that of the company's guides. Most people are only too happy to tell you what they've been up to for the last five or fifty years. You should also find out if the company is insured and if the guides have first-aid certification. Even on the "safest" trip, the unexpected can happen—if it couldn't, there would be no sense in going. Find out, too, just what is expected of you as a customer—what experience you should have, what clothing or equipment you should bring along, and if there are any requirements in regard to the physical condition of participants. Anybody in reasonably good health can go on most of these trips, but some do require a high level of competence in selected skills, such as downhill skiing on heli-skiing trips. Ask about group discounts, special rates for children, or off-season or midweek rates. You have the right to ask these questions—remember, it's your time and money being invested, and a good operator will appreciate your honest interest.

The prices listed in this guidebook are based on anticipated rates for the 1981 season and are as exact as our publication date allows. Cost is per person unless otherwise noted and usually includes food and the group equipment necessary to carry out the trip. In most cases, it is the customer's responsibility to provide personal gear such as a sleeping bag and tent. For trips based in British Columbia, we have indicated whether the fees are based on Canadian or United States funds by designating "Cdn." or "U.S." after the cost, unless the information was not available. If a "TA" follows the trip description, it means the trip is commissionable through most travel agents. Many operators require a deposit well in advance of their trips, so be sure to ask about cancellation policies in case your plans have to be changed.

There are hundreds of trip options listed in The Northwest Adventure Guide. We hope you have a chance to experience at least one, and we hope that it gives you a greater understanding of and appreciation for the incredible richness of experience available in the Northwest. We've enjoyed putting this guidebook together; we hope you enjoy using it.

# BACKPACKING

Sometimes it seems that everyone in the Northwest owns a backpack, and that taking a weekend hike is as common as a trip to the beach is in southern California. And it's no wonder. The coastal states, Idaho, and British Columbia are blessed with some of the most varied terrain on the continent, and wilderness is only a couple of hours away at most.

A great deal of the enthusiasm for backpacking stems from the fact that it is relatively inexpensive and requires only a few pieces of specialized equipment. Sturdy hiking boots with lug soles, suitable for nearly all kinds of trails, come in a variety of styles and costs. Small portable stoves weigh less than two pounds. Tents, once just confining, heavy A-frames, have been freed of guy lines, straight lines, and even rain flies in the last decade as new fabrics and dome designs have been developed. Sleeping bags of various styles and fills are designed for all sorts of weather conditions. And the backpack itself is today made of lightweight aluminum, nylon cloth, and carefully thought-out systems of belts and straps for maximum balance and comfort. A pack, a sleeping bag, a tent, a stove, and a good pair of boots—that's the basic equipment, and it can take you anywhere, from the spectacular heights of the Canadian Rockies to the narrow beaches at the base of California's coastal cliffs.

One of the most surprising things about backpacking is that it's not simply a mountain sport. Sure, there are the high alpine lakes of the North Cascades, the rugged Sawtooths in Idaho, and the impressive rock spires of Yosemite. But there also are the verdant valleys of the Willamette Forest; trails along the Rogue, Columbia, and Snake rivers; and miles of wild, uninhabited coastline along Vancouver Island's west coast.

For those interested in natural history, backpacking is the best way to get a first-hand education. The ongoing process of the earth's growth is made clear by visiting Mount Edziza in British Columbia, where volcanic landscapes graphically demonstrate the creation of terrain through cataclysmic action. Mountain goats that have never known the crack of a hunter's rifle scramble over the rocks in the high interior of Washington's Olympic Peninsula. Bald eagles nest near the coastal fjords of British Columbia's Inside Passage. It is, indeed, an education to camp in the natural world, a lesson in how the earth has operated for millenia and operates still far from the often meddlesome curiosity of human society.

So why take an organized trip into the wilderness? Why not just go it alone, with a couple of friends, for an overnighter to your favorite mountain or lake? Consider the advantages of taking a backpacking adventure trip with a guide. A guide knows not only the geologic history of the land but also its human history: the stories of miners who came into

the hills in search of gold, silver, or precious stones, and who rarely suc-
ceeded; the trappers who lived for years in a wild and lonely forest; the
native Americans who once hunted in these woods, fished in these rivers,
and told their children how Raven stole fire from the sun and brought it
to warm the hearths.

Then there are the other, more practical lessons, that a wilderness
guide can teach. Such trail techniques as map reading, personal energy
conservation, and foot care must be learned in order to experience safe
independent hikes later on. Even the more aesthetic aspects of backcountry travel call for an experienced hand to relay knowledge. For example,
a guide can teach you how to get good photographs by adjusting to compensate for exposures in bright snow, by knowing when to use depth of
field and when to isolate your focal plane, or by understanding when to
stop the movement of a stream cascading over rocks and when to let the
flow itself be the subject of the composition. For art and education, soli-
tude and companionship, physical challenge and relaxation, guided
backpacking in the Northwest is the way to go.

# British Columbia

Roger Griffiths, Alpine Crafts Ltd., 1286 Kingsway, Vancouver, B.C., Canada V5V 3E1; (604)873-4915. Eight-day trips take hikers to remote areas, including Mt. Waddington and the West Coast Trail, during spring and summer months. Cost: $200.

David Dalby, Alpine Kamping Ltd., P.O. Box 217, Valemount, B.C., Canada V0E 2Z0; (604)566-4477. Three- or 4-day guided trips into the Canadian Rockies or the Cariboo or Monashee ranges following 2 or 3 days of training trips and recreational activities. Trips offered from June to October, with camping and inn accommodations. Cost: $497. (TA)

John Carter, Arnica Adventure, R.R. 1, Nelson, B.C., Canada V1L 5P4; (604) 825-9351. Five- and 7-day trips begin with a helicopter ride or hike to a remote base camp from which day-hikes are made. Camps feature individual tent accommodations, homemade meals, and spectacular mountain scenery. Trips offered from July to September. Cost: $235(Cdn.) for 5-day trips, $335 for 7-day trips.

Brian McDonald, Black Tusk Touring and Guide Service Ltd., 3064 St. Kildas Ave., N. Vancouver, B.C., Canada V7N 2A9; (604) 985-9223. Two-week trip to Mt. Edziza in August to photograph volcanic landscapes. Cost: $785.

Trekspeditions Adventure Travel, Ecosummer Canada, 207 W. Hastings St., suite 304, Vancouver, B.C., Canada V6B 1H7; (604)688-3921. Several trips lasting 11 days to 2 weeks to Mt. Edziza and surrounding plateau, the Spatsizi Provincial Park, and Mt. Robson. Emphasis on exploration, natural history, and acquisition of wilderness skills. Trips offered from July through September. Cost: $400-650, from Smithers. (TA)

Arnör Larson, Northern Lights Alpine Recreation, Box 399, Invermere, B.C., Canada V0A 1K0; (604)342-6042. Eight-day alpine hiking trips from July to October on and off trails in the Canadian Rockies. Side trips and minor peak scrambles undertaken if group wishes. Hikers must provide their own food and equipment. Cost: $125-175(Cdn.).

Pacific Northwest Sea Trails, Inc., 12522 Montecito Rd., Seal Beach, CA 90740; (213) 594-8347. Eight- and 14-day land and sea trips to coastal fjords of the Inside Passage emphasize wilderness skills and interpersonal growth. Water travel by inflatable boat; land travel by foot. Trips offered from June to August. Cost: $225 for 8-day trips, $400 for 14-day trips, from Campbell River. (TA)

Jim or Myrna Boulding, Strathcona Park Lodge and Outdoor Education Centre, Box 2160, Campbell River, B.C., Canada V9W 5C9; Campbell River radio, Strathcona Lodge 59 7021. A variety of 1- to 10-day trips to different areas in Strathcona Park and Nootka Sound for photography and learning local history and wilderness skills. Cost: $40-320 (Cdn.). (TA)

Bernie or Swede Gano, Tee Slash Dee Ranch, Anahim Lake, B.C., Canada V0L 1C0; Williams Lake radio, Chilanko channel, 8-L71. Custom backpack trips for small groups from wilderness working ranch. Cost: $75-80/day.

# Washington

Loren Foss, Aerie Northwest, 4558 4th N.E., Seattle, WA 98105; (206)634-2849. Multi-weekend field courses in alpine travel for beginning backpackers and in winter camping, in mountain areas around Seattle. Wilderness skills taught in evening sessions with practical experience over 4 weekends. Winter-camping courses offered from January to March, alpine travel courses from April to June. Week-long hikes in the Olympics and the Pasayten Wilderness also offered in summer. Cost: $170-175 for courses, $140-160 for hikes.

**David Birkner, American Field Studies, 2301 W. Raye St., Seattle, WA 98199; (206)282-2301.** Many hiking trips offered in the Pacific Northwest, including special trips for beginners, women, and the handicapped. Trips are led by naturalist-guides and emphasize natural environment, flora and fauna, and ecology. College credit is available. Cost: $75 for 2-day trips, $179 for 3-day trips. (TA)

**Folkways International Trekking, Inc., Box 68484, Oak Grove, OR 97268; (503) 653-5882.** The only Sherpa-led trekking program in the U.S. includes 8- to 18-day treks to explore ghost towns or alpine country. Some programs focus on botanical or geological aspects of the Northwest. Cost: available upon request.

**Eric Sanford, Liberty Bell Alpine Tours, Mazama, WA 98833; (509)996-2250.** Several 5-day trips offered from June to September in the North Cascades, Olympic National Park, and the Glacier Peak Wilderness; 12-day trek on the Pacific Crest Trail offered in July and August. Hikes are leisurely and reflect hikers' interests and abilities. Composite trips, combining such activities as biking, rafting, and hiking, are also offered. Cost: $175 for 5-day trips, $430 for 12-day trip. (TA)

**Lance Young, Northwest Recreational Outing Club, 5601 N.E. 77th, Seattle, WA 98115; (206)784-3534 or 523-5414.** One-day and overnight weekend trips to alpine lakes and ghost towns in the Cascade Mountains by way of historic mining trails. Evening meetings provide orientation. Cost: $11, plus $15 annual membership fee.

**Olympic Adventures, P.O. Box 2135, Forks, WA 98331; (206)374-6090 or 2237.** Weekend and 5-day trips to ocean beaches, the rain forest, and the high country of Olympic National Park from May to September. Trips planned for individuals and families of varying hiking abilities. A 5-day trip combines hiking with canoeing across Lake Ozette. Cost: $65 for weekend trips, $195 for 5-day trips.

**Jeff Utz, Outdoor Adventures, Box 500, Gold Bar, WA 98251; (206)282-8887 or 793-1166.** Three- and 5-day trips into areas of the Olympic and Cascade ranges accessible only by trail. Side trips from base camps include such activities as wildflower indentification, fishing, photography, and watching for mountain goats and black bear. Trips offered from June to August. Wilderness day-hikes especially suited for groups offered year-round. Cost: $139 for 3-day trips, $198 for 5-day trips, $17 for day-hikes.

**David Button, Pacific Northwest Float Trips, 829 Waldron St., Sedro Woolley, WA 98284; (206)855-0535.** Base camp in the Washington wilderness allows for day-hikes to view wildflowers, explore the mountain environment, and fish. Camp location is moved weekly. Cost: $50/day. (TA)

# Oregon

**David Birkner, American Field Studies, 2301 W. Raye St., Seattle, WA 98199; (206)282-4878.** See Washington listing.

**Richard Arend, Exploregon, 9603 S.W. Taylor, Portland, OR 98105; (206) 634-2849.** Trips lasting 1 to 4 days to various areas in the Oregon wilderness, including a 36-mile loop around Mt. Hood, an exploration of the glacier fields of Mt. Jefferson, an easy hike to lakes in the Mt. Hood National Forest, and day-hikes to the Columbia River Gorge. Some trips planned especially for families. Guides impart knowledge of botany, geology, first aid, and folklore. Cost: $120 for 2-day trips, $240 for 4-day trips. (TA)

Folkways International Trekking, Inc., Box 68484, Oak Grove, OR 97268; (503) 653-5882. See Washington listing.

Ed Johann, Johann Mountain Guides, P.O. Box 2334, Lincoln City, OR 97367; (503)996-3232. Two- to 10-day hikes, including a 7- to 10-day trek on the Oregon Coast Trail, featuring bivouacs on the beach and abundant wildlife. Activities include photography, fishing, beachcombing, and learning survival techniques. Cost: $35/day. (TA)

Julia Porter or Marcia Munson, Keep Listening Wilderness Trips for Women, P.O. Box 446, Sandy, OR 97055; (503) 239-6896. Four- to 8-day trips designed for all levels of backpacking ability offered from May to September. Trips focus on learning wilderness skills and have supportive, noncompetitive atmosphere. Cost: $35-280, depending on income.

Outing Dept., Sierra Club, 530 Bush St., San Francisco, CA 94108; (415)981-8634. Conservation-conscious trips of 6 to 10 days in wilderness areas in summer. Most trips include 1 or more layover days for relaxing, swimming, or individual exploration. Trips range in difficulty from leisurely to strenuous; they are run cooperatively, with all participants sharing in chores. Some trips offered especially for teens. Cost: $105-175.

# Idaho

Bob Liming, Alpine Wilderness Leadership School, 1801 Burrell Ave., Lewiston, ID 83501; (208)743-2478. Six-day trip along the Snake River for reasonably fit senior citizens. Trip begins with boat ride to Johnson Bar, then continues at an unhurried pace by foot for 19 miles downstream. Trip offered in April. Cost: $375.

Lyman C. Dye, EE-DA-HOW Mountaineering and Guide Service, P.O. Box 207, Ucon, ID 83454; (208)523-9276. Seven days amid the Sawtooth peaks enjoying their flora, lakes and streams, and wildlife and learning their historical and geological background. Trips offered from July to September. Cost: $280.

Bob or Jan Sevy, Sevy Guide Service, Box 1527, Sun Valley, ID 83353; (208) 788-3440. Combination backpacking and river-rafting trips along the Middle Fork of the Salmon River, or on the Snake River and in Hells Canyon offered on a charter basis. Trips last 7 days and feature high mountain trails, alpine lakes, and fresh trout on the campfire menu. Cost: $600.

Outing Dept., Sierra Club, 530 Bush St., San Francisco, CA 94108; (415)981-8634. See Oregon listing.

Bill Mason, The Snug Co., Box 598, Sun Valley, ID 83353; (208)622-9305. Guided overnight trips available in Sun Valley area by arrangement. Cost: $50-90, depending on group size, includes food, transportation, and guide service.

The Tonsmeires, Wilderness River Outfitters and Trail Expeditions, Inc., P.O. Box 871, Salmon, ID 83467; (208)756-3959. Five- to 9-day trips in the White Cloud Peaks of the Sawtooth National Recreation Area offered in August. Trips are leisurely, with longer, more strenuous trips available by special request. Company provides basic backpacking gear. Cost: $320 for 5-day trips, $560 for 8-day trips. (TA)

Daril or Chris Petersen, Wilderness Trails, P.O. Box 9252, Moscow, ID 83843; (208)882-1955. Six- and 10-day trips in and around the River of No Return Wilderness offered from May to September. Two-week trips in May and October. Trips are planned according to hikers' abilities and interests, and trail techniques and outdoor skills are taught. Cost: $280 for 6-day trips, $380 for 10-day trips, $510 for 2-week trips, from McCall.

# California

Ken Hanley, Adventure Unique, 19 Washington St., Santa Clara, CA 95050; (408)243-4878. Two-, 3-, and 7-day trips in the High Sierra Nevada, or along the Monterey coast or other northern California beaches. Trips begin with a 2- to 8-mile hike to a base camp, from which hikers can explore on their own or fish for trout. Cost: $49 for 2-day trips, $63 for 3-day trips, $98 for 7-day trips.

George Armstrong, All-Outdoors Adventure Trips, 2151 San Miguel Dr., Walnut Creek, CA 94596; (415)934-0240. Four-day trip to the Emigrant Basin area and a 6-day trip to the high country above Yosemite Valley in summer. Improvement of wilderness skills emphasized; all levels of backpacking experience welcome. Cooking and clean-up responsibilities are shared by the group. Five-day combination river-rafting and backpacking trips for teens offered in July and August. Cost: $105 for 4-day trip, $160 for 6-day trip, $195 for teen trips.

Terry Halbert, Mountain People School, 157 Oak Spring Dr., San Anselmo, CA 94960; (415)457-3664. Week-long trips in the Sierra Nevada from June to September to introduce a variety of wilderness skills, including map reading, first aid, and campcraft. Similar 2-week trips feature diet of natural wild foods, experience in group leadership, and rock climbing. Cost: $150 for 1-week trips, $280 for 2-week trips.

Outing Dept., Sierra Club, 530 Bush St., San Francisco, CA 94108; (415)981-8634. See Oregon listing.

Dottie Moore or Mike McCoy, Wilderness Extension, University Extension, University of California, Davis, CA 95616; (916)752-3098. Six-week backpacking first-aid course consisting of evening sessions and a weekend field trip. Program covers shock and respiratory emergencies, hypothermia, poisonings, altitude sickness, and bone injuries. Participants must provide own equipment and first-aid materials and share food expenses. Cost: $70, includes instruction and college credit.

# BALLOONING

It was almost 200 years ago, in 1783, that the first manned hot-air balloon went aloft over the countryside of France. For a time thereafter, ballooning was heralded as the transportation of the future and was even used in warfare on surveillance missions. While more technologically advanced means of flight became prominent in the twentieth century and ballooning abruptly faded from favor, it retained the earlier era's charm, grace, and aesthetic quality that are so missing from modern transportation. The peaceful experience of silently drifting in these brightly colored globes, floating at nature's pace, is one that people more used to airplanes and jets often choose as a favorite diversion.

Commercial balloon trips usually last for at least an hour, depending on the weather and wind conditions. They go aloft as early in the morning as possible, since the heat of later day generates stronger, less predictable winds. Propane burners are used to inflate the nylon balloons with heated air, and a carriage of wicker, steel, and suede is the most common vehicle in which passengers ride. Although the early-morning flight time sometimes makes warm clothing advisable, no special precautions in dress need be taken. Tennis or running shoes are recommended because they are lightweight and prevent slipping on the floor of the carriage, while layers of jackets, sweaters, and shirts can be removed as the day warms up.

Because FAA regulations prevent flying a balloon in clouds or heavy fog, the view from the skies usually is extraordinarily clear. This view not only provides a breathtaking perspective on the earth below, but also gives photographers an opportunity for some unusual shots. For pictures of the balloon, carriage, and occupants, a wide-angle lens is necessary. A telephoto lens is helpful for picking out the specifics of the landscape below, such as creeks winding through forests, old farmhouses, the symmetrical patterns of vineyards, or even the urgent, earthbound arterials of automobiles over which the balloon floats, silent and aloof.

Although commercial ballooning has been around for years, in few other areas of the country has it caught on as it has in the gently rolling counties around San Francisco. Perhaps this is because of the weather, usually clear away from the fog-shrouded bay and warm enough year-round to allow an enjoyable morning adventure. Then again, it could well be because of the picturesque beauty of the Sonoma, Napa, and San Joaquin valleys where most balloon trips are offered. Some flights even ride the breezes over the Coast Range west of San Jose, toward the broad blue surface of Monterey Bay.

The Puget Sound region of western Washington is a fascinating area to survey from above. Broad lakes of fresh water stand out in remembrance of the same glacial action that once filled the enormous salt-water sound itself. On either side of this low-lying center, hills rise into two mountain ranges, capped by snowy peaks. Mount Olympus, Mount Constance, and the Brothers appear to crown the Olympics to the west; Glacier Peak, Mount Baker, and Mount Rainier are some that dominate the Cascades to the east.

In easternmost Idaho, the Teton Range rises sharply from a flat valley floor, a perfect setting for balloon flights that offer spectacular views of the mountains within Grand Teton National Park. The Tetons are a classic example of block faulting, which occurs when a section of the earth's crust is slowly thrust upward along the sharp edge of a fault line. From the air, the abrupt flanks of the Tetons—capped by the 13,766-foot summit of Grand Teton—seem crisscrossed with unintelligible inscriptions, written in snow by a hand that uses the language of geological processes to tell a tale of time.

Modern balloonists try to preserve the traditions of this antique, but not antiquated, sport. For instance, to soothe the shocked farmer onto whose pastures a balloon had dropped, early aeronauts carried bottles of champagne on every flight. This practice, thankfully, has endured to this day, as nearly all commercial flights end with a toast to the passengers, new converts to modern hot-air ballooning.

# Washington

William Kelso, The Great Northwest Aerial Navigation Co., 7616 79th Ave. S.E., Mercer Island, WA 98040; (206) 232-2023. Year-round weekend ascensions of 1 to 2 hours terminating with champagne brunch or hors d'oeuvres depending on time of day. Balloon has largest passenger carriage in the Pacific Northwest. Shorter flights offered during the week. Tethered rides, charters, and instruction also available. Cost: $150/couple on weekends, $45/person on weekdays, $5 for tethered rides. (TA)

# Idaho

Fred Reed, Red Baron Flying Service, Teton Peaks Airport, Driggs, ID 83422; (208)354-8131. One-hour flights in the Teton Valley year-round terminating with a champagne toast. Flight instruction and tethered flights also offered. Cost: $58. (TA)

# California

Kathy Kyle, Aerostat Renaissance, A Ballooning Company, P.O. Box 3536, Napa, CA 94558; (707)255-6356. One-hour flights over the Napa Valley, followed by a champagne toast, offered year-round at sunrise. Promotional flights, fund-raisers, and pilot instruction also available. Cost: $90.

Brent Stockwell or Christine Kalakuka, Balloon Excelsior, Inc., 1241 High St., Oakland, CA 94601; (415)261-4222. One-hour flights at dawn in the San Joaquin

Valley or Livermore area, followed by a champagne toast. Flights offered daily year-round. Flight instruction also available. Cost: $175 for 2 persons, $225 for 3, $260 for 4.

**Don or Rita Wilson, Cloud Pleasers Balloon Co., 816 Colusa, Berkeley, CA 94707; (415)524-3953 or 5 CLOUD 4.** Balloon flights over the Napa Valley on clear, calm weekend days. Trips followed by champagne brunch. Cost: $75.

**Ken O'Connor, 194th Aerostat Squadron, 1110 San Pedro Ave., Morgan Hill, CA 95037; (408)779-4462.** Half-hour to 2-hour flights offered daily year-round, including a 2-hour flight over the Coast Range with spectacular views of the countryside, and a dawn flight ascending in the predawn darkness and landing at dawn, both followed by a champagne brunch. Shorter flights include a champagne toast. Teth-

ered 30-foot ascensions also available. Cost: $50 for ½-hour flights, $90 for 1-hour flights, $275 for Coast Range or dawn flights, $11 for tethered flights. (TA)

**Bob Linde, Sunrise Balloon, P.O. Box 6757, Santa Rosa, CA 95406; (707) 542-5781.** Balloon flights offered over the wine country of the Sonoma and Napa valleys year-round. Flights are followed by a champagne toast; champagne brunch available on request at extra charge. Cost: $50 for ½-hour flights, $90 for 1-hour flights.

**Mick or Sally Vale, Balloon Ascension Division, Vale Enterprises, 20852 Elenda Dr., Cupertino, CA 95014; (408)446-2793.** Two-hour flights offered year-round. Each trip ends with a wine-tasting tour of the antique aircraft museum in Cupertino. Flight instruction and custom trips also available. Cost: $150 for 2 persons. (TA)

# BICYCLING

If the great gas crunch of the seventies continues into the eighties, the whole style of vacationing in America may change. Indeed, some changes are already apparent. Bicycle vacations have become an increasingly popular way to see much of the Northwest, and pedalers are finding that, compared with driving, the slower pace of bicycle travel, the greater attention to local detail, and the more rigorous involvement with the terrain are giving them an informative, inexpensive, and physically rewarding experience.

Bicycle trips are usually arranged for relatively small groups—twenty people is an average. A guide or two is on hand to explain the local lore and lead the way down backcountry roads as well as to help with necessary repairs and maintenance. Usually, fewer than forty miles a day are covered, even when the local attractions outweigh the impulse to travel onward. In California, for instance, cycling the Silverado Trail in Sonoma County offers many enchanting diversions, the foremost of which is the sampling of varietal wines in the tasting rooms of some of America's finest wineries.

Those who have never taken an extended bicycle trip may think of it as only tortuous climbs up endless hills, alternating with exhilarating downhill coasts. In fact, a long trip offers many opportunities for different sorts of activities, and variety is a major priority for most tour planners. A day of canoeing may be scheduled on a crystal-clear lake; hikes up to alpine meadows might lead to sightings of mule deer, mountain goats, or even a far-off black bear. Near the coast, marine life is a highlight; in major cities and towns, cultural attractions and good cuisine are spotlighted. British Columbia tours offer all these activities in visits to such areas as the Gulf Islands, the city of Vancouver, and Jasper or Banff national parks.

Then there's the weather, which creates a few surprises of its own. It might rain cats and dogs one day and pour nothing but sunshine the next. This makes packing for a bike trip especially challenging because most of the gear—including sleeping bag and tent on overnight trips—must fit in the saddle bags or pannier of a ten-speed bicycle. (Of course, a supply van usually is available to carry community camping gear and to offer a lift to a road-weary pedaler.) Nylon rain gear is lightweight and useful, and wool clothing retains its insulating qualities even when the weather is wet—as it so often is near the Pacific coast. On the other hand, many people find it most comfortable to cycle in shorts, and a bathing suit is handy for dips in hot springs, lakes, or the ocean itself.

The attractions of cycling in the Northwest are many, but most visitors find the wild coasts of Washington, Oregon, and northern California especially well suited to exploration by bicycle. Virgin forests sweep out of the coastal ranges to stop only at the water's edge; sheer promontories drop hundreds of feet into the boiling surf; and rocky outcroppings jut into the blue ocean, offering roosts to seabirds and sea lions. On the other hand, there are the scenic country roads, the small towns that time seems to have forgotten, and the quiet river campsites and rolling farmlands of the inland, such as the Willamette Valley in central Oregon.

The itinerary on longer trips often varies from one outing to the next, since the participants have many varied interests in the countryside they are exploring. One trip may evolve into a bird-watching expedition; another may include hours of lounging on the sandy beaches, deepening tans; still another may focus on the forgotten history of the area, with stops at all the small roadside attractions, museums, missions, and novelty stores. Perhaps more than any other type of vacation, a bicycle trip is what you make of it. And all it takes is two wheels, good health, curiosity, and determination.

# British Columbia

Tom Heavey, The Biking Expedition, Inc., P.O. Box 547, Henniker, NH 03242; (603)428-7500. A bicycle-camping trip for 13- to 18-year-olds lasting 34 days in June and July. The trip begins in Vancouver, British Columbia, continues on to the San Juan Islands and through northern British Columbia, and ends in Calgary, Alberta. Opportunity for swimming, clamming, and exploring Vancouver, quaint fishing villages, and Jasper and Banff national parks. Cost: $1,107 from eastern U.S. (arrangements can be made to meet the group in Vancouver.).

Julia Porter or Marcia Munson, Keep Listening Wilderness Trips for Women, P.O. Box 446, Sandy, OR 97055; (503)239-6896. Four- and 7-day bicycle-camping trips offered from May through August. All trips include instruction in biking techniques and bike repair and maintenance as well as such outdoor skills as campsite selection and outdoor cooking. Time is allowed for such activities as photography and swimming. Cost: $35-125 for 4-day trips, $100-275 for 7-day trips, depending on income.

Mary Jane Barnes, Rocky Mountain Cycle Tours, P.O. Box 895, Banff, Alta. Canada T0L 0C0; (403)762-3477. Two-week camping trips in the British Columbia Lake District from June to August. Cyclists help with food buying and preparation and have opportunity for hiking, swimming in the lakes, and attending bicycle maintenance clinics. Cost: $300. (TA)

Sandra duBrule, Safari Expeditions, Ltd., 969 W. Broadway, Vancouver, B.C., Canada V5Z 1K3; (604)738-5917. Seven-day trips begin in Vancouver, British Columbia, visit Orcas and Lopez islands in the San Juans, and end in Victoria on Vancouver Island. Time for exploring, fishing, swimming, and sunbathing. Trips offered from May to August; bicycles provided. Cost: $360(Cdn.).

# Washington

Tom Hale or Linda Petty, Backroads Bicycle Touring Co., 6122 Margarido Dr., Oakland, CA 94618; (415)652-0786. Weekend and week-long bicycle tours from March through October emphasizing rediscovery of nature. People of all ages and levels of cycling experience are welcome; tours are carefully planned but not regimented, so each participant can select the degree of challenge desired. Custom-tailored trips are also available. Cost: $350 for 6-day tours. (TA)

Keith Nelson, Excursions Extraordinaires, 1452 Rainier Dr., Tacoma, WA 98466. Four- and 5-day trips around Puget Sound, including a day of sailing in the San Juan Islands, offered in June and July. A relaxed, unhurried pace is taken; each participant is free to determine his or her own riding schedule. Cost: $150. (TA)

Fred Strong, Northwest Bicycle Touring Society, 3411 77th Pl. S.E., Mercer Island, WA 98040; (206)232-7311. Four different inexpensive trips offered in Puget Sound area from May to October. Areas include Mt. Rainier, Orcas Island, and the Olympic Peninsula. Forty to 60 miles are covered each day. Cost: $17-19 for 2- and 3-day trips.

# Oregon

Gerhard Meng, Gerhard's Bicycle Odysseys, 1137 S.W. Yamhill, Portland, OR 97205; (503)223-2402. Week-long trip along the Oregon coast offered in July. Average daily distance of 39 miles allows time for side trips. Package includes lodging, most meals, welcome party, and sag wagon. Cost: $475. (TA)

Julia Porter or Marcia Munson, **Keep Listening Wilderness Trips for Women,** P.O. Box 446, Sandy, OR 97055; (503) 239-6896. See British Columbia listing.

# California

Ken Hanley, **Adventure Unique,** 19 Washington St., Santa Clara, CA 95050; (408)243-4878. Weekend or 3-day bicycle-camping tours of 20 to 35 miles a day in the High Sierra Nevada or along the Russian River and the coastline. Cost: $49 for weekend trips, $63 for 3-day trips.

George Armstrong, **All-Outdoors Adventure Trips,** 2151 San Miguel Dr., Walnut Creek, CA 94596; (415)934-0240. Two-day trips from Mendocino to the Russian River and 4-day trips in the Sierra Nevada in July and September. Two-day trips include a tour of the Yosemite Valley; on 4-day trips, crew dives for abalone for dinner. Sag wagon available for tired cyclists. Cost: $75 for 2-day trips, $130 for 4-day trips. (TA)

Tom Hale or Linda Petty, **Backroads Bicycle Touring Co.,** 6122 Margarido Dr., Oakland, CA 94618; (415)652-0786. See Washington listing.

# CANOEING

It was probably through watching trees felled by high winds or floods drift downstream on a river's current that people hit upon the notion of the prototypal canoe. In some parts of the world, such as New Zealand, the Caribbean, and the Northwest, hollowed-out logs or dugouts were used in warfare, in commerce, and for simple transportation. Here in the Northwest, Salish, Haida, and Nootka Indians used vessels over fifty feet long on the open sea to stalk hair seals, porpoises, and even whales. Elsewhere, as in New England, bark was stretched over wooden frames to create faster, more elegant craft.

Today's canoes, though lighter and more durable, differ little from these original designs, but their value has been extended from the exclusively pragmatic sphere to include the recreational. They are usually made of aluminum, fiberglass, or ABS—a rigid foam sandwiched between two layers of high-impact plastic. Inflatable models are also available for canoeing that is not technically exacting or for training. Most open canoes are about fourteen to seventeen feet long and less than a yard wide amidships. Using wood, plastic, or aluminum paddles, two people maneuver the canoe with different strokes, including high and low braces, backpaddles, and the J-stroke. Winding through rocks, waves, and eddies in white water is more demanding than canoeing on flat water, for the long length of the craft makes it relatively easy to tip.

Although a number of canoeing courses are available, it is on extended trips that the real benefits of the sport can be realized. Five days to two weeks spent near the Yukon River in the British Columbia wilderness, along the wooded Vancouver Island coast, or on the upper Columbia River are rich with wildlife sightings and rugged scenery. Trips in Washington's Olympic National Park combine canoeing on Lake Ozette with hiking to the coastline at Cape Alava. The Eel and Trinity rivers, among the most beautiful and least crowded in California, offer their waters for both training and camping during the spring, summer, and fall. Few other sports provide both the novice and expert with the peace of outdoor living combined with a link to a regional heritage.

# British Columbia

Ken Hanley, Adventure Unique, 19 Washington St., Santa Clara, CA 95050; (408)243-4878. Ten days of touring British Columbia by canoe in September, designed to be a learning experience in outdoor skills

and the natural environment. Special programs can be designed for groups and organizations. Cost: $670.

John D. Carter, Arnica Adventure, R.R.1, Nelson, B.C., Canada V1L 5P4; (604) 825-9351. Five-day trips on Slocan Lake, a large mountain lake nestled between the Valhalla and Slocan ranges, June through August; and 5-day trips on the upper Columbia River, one of British Columbia's best wildfowl areas, in May and September. Time for swimming, fishing, hiking, and exploring. Cost: $230(Cdn.) for Slocan Lake trips, $250 for Columbia River trips. (TA)

Trekspeditions Adventure Travel, Eco-summer Canada, 207 W. Hastings St., suite 304, Vancouver, B.C., Canada V6B 1H7; (604)688-3921. Twelve-day trip in Bowron Lake Park, which has a unique circuit of 10 lakes, in the heart of the Cariboos. Wildlife is protected and thus abundant in the park; emphasis is given to photography and ecological study. Trip departs from Prince George. Cost: $435. (TA)

Ev Woodward or Eileen Broomell, The Lodge, Inc., Box 86, Ashford, WA 98304; (206)569-2312. Five- to 13-day wilderness trips with environmental and historical-background orientation. Side trips for nature exploration. Paddling skills and above average physical condition required. Canoe instruction also offered throughout western Washington. Cost: $200-480.

Bruce Johnson, North Country Travelers, Box 14, Atlin, B.C., Canada V0W 1A0; (604)651-7679. Combination canoe/hiking trips in wilderness area of northern British Columbia, based at wilderness homestead on the Atlin River. Opportunity for wildlife observation and photography. Activities planned according to guests' interests. Cost: $110/day. (TA)

Robert Herman, Northwest Waters, Box 212C, Portland, OR 97207;(503)244-0024. Thirteen-day trips to observe wildlife and marine life of islands and seashore of

Vancouver Island's west coast from June through September. Company provides equipment and lodging but not food. No experience necessary. Cost: $285.

**Outing Dept., Sierra Club, 530 Bush St., San Francisco, CA 94108; (415)981-8634.** Seven- to 12-day outings in wilderness areas in summer. Participants paddle craft with advice and instruction from leader. Special family trips, for families with at least one teenager, also offered. Paddling skills required vary, but swimming ability is required for all. Cost: $195-375.

**Jim or Myrna Boulding, Strathcona Park Lodge and Outdoor Education Centre, Box 2160, Campbell River, B.C., Canada V9W 5C9; Campbell River radio, Strathcona Lodge 59 7021.** Several canoe trips

on west coast of Vancouver Island, including ocean-canoeing trips in Kyuquot Sound, camping trips in Nootka Sound, and trips encompassing west coast lakes, rivers, and ocean. Courses in basic canoeing skills and white-water canoeing, as well as courses leading to instructor certification, also offered. Cost: $360(Cdn.) for Kyuquot Sound trips, $320 for Nootka Sound trips, $335 for lakes, rivers, and ocean trips. (TA)

# Washington

**Ev Woodward or Eileen Broomell, The**

skills on Lake Wenatchee; evenings are spent in discussion of various aspects of the sport. Lodging and meals are provided in an inn on the shores of Lake Wenatchee or students can choose to camp. Round-trip transportation from Seattle is available. Also offered are classes in Seattle that meet on 4 weekday evenings and a weekend, and graduate overnight trips. Cost: $320 for Wenatchee camps, $125 for Seattle classes.

# Oregon

Outing Dept., Sierra Club, 530 Bush St., San Francisco, CA 94108; (415)981-8634. See British Columbia listing.

# California

Ann Dwyer, California Rivers, P.O. Box 468, Geyserville, CA 95441; (707)857-3872. Canoe trips on the Eel and Trinity rivers in summer with wilderness camping on the river banks. Opportunity for hiking. Paddling skills needed for Trinity River trips. Cost: $150 for Eel River trips, $180 for Trinity River trips.

Alan Ehrgott or Butch Carber, Pacific Adventures, Box 5041, Riverside CA 92517; (714)684-1227. Weekend trips on the Russian River in spring. Includes round-trip transportation from San Francisco, meals, equipment, and informal instruction. No experience required. Cost: $110. (TA)

Outing Dept., Sierra Club, 530 Bush St., San Francisco, CA 94108; (415)981-8634. See British Columbia listing.

William Trowbridge, Trowbridge Recreation Inc., 20 Healdsburg Ave.,

Lodge, Inc., Box 86, Ashford, WA 98304; (206)569-2312. See British Columbia listing.

Olympic Adventures Inc., P.O. Box 2135, Forks, WA 98331; (206)374-6090. Five-day combination canoeing/backpacking trips in summer on the Olympic Peninsula, including 2 days of canoeing on Ozette Lake, and hiking through the rain forest to the ocean beach. Two-day canoe trips on weekends in summer also offered. Cost: $195 for combination trips.

Doug Baker, White Water Sports, 307 N.E. 71st, Seattle, WA 98115; (206) 523-5150. Week-long canoeing camps in Wenatchee in summer. Daily trips on the White, Chiwawa, Wenatchee, and Skykomish rivers follow instruction in basic

Healdsburg, CA 95448; (707)433-7247.
One- and 2-day self-guided trips on the
Russian and American rivers. Four- and
5-day packages available for groups.
Cost: $22/canoe for 1 day, $30/canoe for
2 days, $35-40/canoe for 4 or 5 days;
$2/person/night for camping. (TA)

Dottie Moore or Mike McCoy, Wilderness Extension, University Extension,
University of California, Davis, CA
95616; (916)752-3098. Introduction to
river canoeing course and wilderness canoeing course offered on spring weekends. Introductory course is held on Nim-
bus Lake and the American River, wilderness canoeing course on the Rubicon
River. Introductory course or consent of
instructor required for wilderness canoeing course. Cost: $55 for introductory
course, $125 for wilderness canoeing
course.

O.K. or Glenna Goodwin, World of
Whitewater, P.O. Box 708, Big Bar, CA
96010; (916)623-6588 or 4110. One-day,
weekend, or five-day canoeing clinics for
all levels of skill offered March through
October. Custom-tailored group training
programs also available. Training takes
place on Trinity River. Cost: $100 for
weekend clinics, $250 for 5-day clinics.

# CROSS-COUNTRY SKIING

Anyone who has spent any time in the woods knows of the changes winter can bring. Terrain is transformed into gentle white curves. Vegetation, from the reticular branching of bare alders to the sturdy constancy of firs, stands out sharply against the snow. Silence frames each whisper of wind in a background of emptiness. Yet life continues on this arresting blanket of snow: odd-shaped ideographs on the forest floor describe the course of creatures like hesitant ptarmigan and wily silver foxes. And the twin-tracked trail of the cross-country skier shows that humans, too, tour the woods in the wintertime.

The United States has few better areas than the Northwest for cross-country skiing. Every type of landscape is accessible, from broad open meadows to rugged mountain ridges that overlook the wild, untracked interior of mile-high mountain ranges. By far the greatest advantage, of course—and the one that has made cross-country skiing so popular—is the isolation of the sport. There's no waiting in line at the lift, no harrowing slalom downhill through the obstacles of novice skiers, no traffic jams in crowded mountain resort parking lots; only the mountains, slowed to the pace of hibernation by the winter's freeze, and the skier.

Of course, there are social advantages to cross-country skiing, too. While you can take five- and six-day expeditions into the remote Tuolumne Meadows above California's Yosemite Valley, you also can make do with day-long jaunts into the woods from comfortable base-camp lodges in the Sierra Nevada or the Cascade, Selkirk, or Purcell mountains. Home cooked meals and an informal family atmosphere often dominate at cross-country lodges, which are set in the midst of quiet valleys and woods.

Then there are the more isolated ski trips. Following groomed snow trails or the untracked backcountry routes, skiers kick and glide from one cabin to the next in the Purcell Range of British Columbia, passing from day to day through an ever-changing variety of landscapes, all made magical by the season. In the Sawtooths of Idaho, the destination might be a yurt, a portable hut based on the ancient design used by nomadic herdsmen of central Asia. Or a snow cave or igloo might be constructed on the spot, using only the materials at hand, to accommodate the tired adventurer for a night in the winter woods.

Many ski tours are open to skiers of any level of experience, since the basic cross-country techniques are readily learned. But for the more advanced skier, whose telemark turn permits gracefully arcing changes of direction on long downhill runs, ski mountaineering beckons. Utilizing a combination of skiing techniques and mountaineering skills, expeditions can be mounted to the highest of peaks even in midwinter. Roped skiing, belaying and rappelling on skis, snow climbing, techniques for long-distance downhill runs are taught and then put to use on winter tours to the High Wallowas in Oregon, the Central Sierra Nevada in California, and the North Cascades in Washington. Whatever the level of skiing required and wherever the tour takes place, expert advice and instruction in avalanche safety and first aid usually are offered.

Most ski tours available in the Northwest include both meals and equipment as well as guides, but a wide variety of packages is available. Some trips provide everything except warm clothes, and some provide nothing except a learned guide. Whatever the options chosen, though, the constants remain—the majesty of the scenery, the challenge of the terrain, the cold, the silence, and the snow.

# British Columbia

Roger Griffiths, Alpine Crafts Ltd., 1286 Kingsway, Vancouver, B.C., Canada V5V 3E1; (604)873-4915. Nordic ski tours of 3 to 4 days for small groups in remote areas of British Columbia. Skiing experience required; trips offered in March and April. Cost: $25/day, includes guide service. (TA)

Batnuni Lake Resorts Ltd., R.R. 5, Gillies Crossing, Quesnel, B.C., Canada V2J 3H9; (206)568-6813. Accommodations in cabins, family-style meals, and rustic conditions for skiers at wilderness lodge in the Euchiniko chain. Many opportunities to see moose, beaver, and wolves. Cost: $36-50(Cdn.)/day, $235-325/week. (TA)

Herb Bleuer, B.C. Powder Guides, P.O. Box 258, Whistler, B.C., Canada V0N 1B0; (604)932-5331 or 894-6994. One week of touring in McGillivray Pass area beginning with helicopter lift to isolated mountain lodge. Trip offered in April. Weekend and custom trips also available. Cost: $360. (TA)

Brad Bradley, Brad's Tours, 401 E. Mercer #31, Seattle, WA 98102; (206)329-0227. Ski package including lodging at Batnuni Lodge from December through March. Over 100 kilometers of wilderness trails; opportunity for wildlife observation. Rental equipment and instruction available. Cost: $290-650(Cdn.)/week. (TA)

Canadian Mountain Holidays Ltd., P.O. Box 1660, Banff, Alta., Canada T0L 0C0; (403)762-4531. Many week-long trips offered in the northern Selkirks and the Canadian Rockies. Trips include alpine, glacier, and cross-country touring and are offered in March and April. Cost: $360-490(Cdn.). (TA)

Bruce Johnson, North Country Travelers, Box 14, Atlin, B.C., Canada V0W 1A0; (604)651-7679. Ski trips in March and April based at a wilderness homestead and sled-dog kennel. Guests learn to drive dogs and are instructed in winter travel and the history of the Canadian north. Cost: $135/day. (TA)

Arnör Larson, Northern Lights Alpine Recreation, Box 399, Invermere, B.C., Canada V0A 1K0; (604)342-6042. Day-tours, glacier tours, and trips out of a base camp available to skiers from November to April. Log cabin serves as a base for trips to alpine meadows, wooded trails, or mountain ridges. Glacier tours cover 30 miles over 2 high passes and several ice fields with opportunities for serious ski mountaineering. Custom trips also available. Cost: $20(Cdn.) for day-tours, $200/week for cabin stays, $250/week for glacier tours.

Repp Agencies, Ptarmigan Tours, 290 Wallinger, Kimberley, B.C., Canada V1A 2E8; (604)427-2221. Week-long ski tours following a string of high-alpine log cabins in the Purcell Range. Maximum group size of 6 allows each tour to be tailored to meet groups' abilities and desires. All tours include wholesome homecooked meals, instruction in cross-country techniques, and spectacular scenery. Trips offered from December to March. Cost: $350/week. (TA)

Jim or Myrna Boulding, Strathcona Park Lodge and Outdoor Education Centre, Box 2160, Campbell River, B.C., Canada V9W 5C9; Campbell River radio, Strathcona Lodge 59 7021. Introduction to cross-country skiing offered on weekends during January for guests at Strathcona Lodge. Course includes instruction in selection and care of equipment, basic techniques, and reading snow conditions. Cost: $65(Cdn.). (TA)

Bernie or Swede Gano, Tee Slash Dee Ranch, Anahim Lake, B.C., Canada V0L 1C0; Williams Lake radio, Chilanko channel, 8-L71. Custom cross-country ski trips from December through March from wilderness working ranch. Cost: $75-80/day.

Craig Pettitt or Grant Copeland, Valhalla

Mountain Touring, Box 284, New Denver, B.C., Canada V0G 1S0; (604)358-7714. Daily and overnight trips into the high country with accommodations in subalpine cabins or in a hostel in New Denver. Tours have informal atmosphere; international meals are featured at hostel. Helicopter arrangements can be made for glacier skiing. Trips offered from November to May. Cost: $60/day.

# Washington

Bill or Peg Stark, Family Adventures, Inc., P.O. Box 312, Leavenworth, WA 98826; (509)548-7330. More than 50 miles of cross-country terrain, from logging roads to ridges and bowls in the Wenatchee National Forest, with camps established for skiers. Guides offer tours along McCue Ridge and to the Scottish Lakes basin. Trails open from November to May, depending on snow. Wholesome, fresh-food meals served in camps. Cost: $20-88/day. (TA)

Eric Sanford, Liberty Bell Alpine Tours, Mazama, WA 98833; (509)996-2250. Five-day inn-to-inn circle tours in the Methow Valley offered from January to March; 5-day telemark ski courses offered for intermediate or advanced skiers in May. Groups are kept very small to ensure individual attention. Cost: $265 for Methow Valley trips, $315 for ski courses.

Van Brinkerhoff, Nordic Mountain, 3320 Meridian Ave. N., Seattle, WA 98103; (206)633-0411. Cross-country skiing into remote and unusual areas in the Cascades, using both uphill and downhill capacity of skis. Offerings include avalanche seminars, snow-camping overnight tours, ski-mountaineering and glacier-skiing trips, and local ski lessons. Skiing from December to June. Cost: $75 for about 15 hours instruction, $40 for snow-camping and avalanche safety seminars, $50 for glacier-skiing trips. (TA)

Dunham Gooding, North Cascades Alpine School, 1212 24th St. W., Bellingham, WA 98225; (206)671-1505. Guided ski-mountaineering expeditions in the North and Central Cascades, in areas such as Nason Ridge and Buffalo and Windy passes. Trips last 5 days, require intermediate to expert skiing ability, and are offered from March to May. Cost: $190.

Lance Young, Northwest Recreational Outing Club, 5601 N.E. 77th, Seattle, WA 98115; (206)784-3534 or 523-5414. Weekend trips from January to March in the North, Central, and South Cascades. Full range of terrain at all destinations. Free lessons are offered for trip participants. Evening courses on related subjects, such as orienteering and avalanche safety, also offered. Cost: $11, plus $15 annual membership fee, includes transportation and instruction. (TA–groups only)

James Moore or Michael Bellert, ORION Expeditions, Inc., 521 N. 72nd, Seattle, WA 98103; (206)782-8928. Two-day cross-country skiing school held in Leavenworth from December to February. Accommodations at bed-and-breakfast lodge; hearty meals provided. Close-knit family atmosphere on trips. Cost: $100. (TA)

Jeff Utz, Outdoor Adventures, Box 500, Gold Bar, WA 98251; (206)282-8887 or

793-1166. Several different trips to the Stevens Pass and Lake Wenatchee areas of the Cascades from December to May. A Bavarian winter weekend is based in Leavenworth, from which day-trips are made; 2-day stay at remote log cabin in the Chiwawa River area is also offered. Bus transportation to program locations and shuttles to trailheads are available. Cost: $48 for 2-day trips; $7 for trailhead shuttle, $17 if guide is included.

**W. Gerald Lynch, Rainier Mountaineering, Inc., 201 St. Helens Ave., Tacoma, WA 98402; (206)627-6242.** Cross-country ski rental and instruction provided on Mt. Rainier on weekends from December to spring. Cost: available upon request. (TA)

**Don Portman, Sun Mountain Lodge, P.O. Box 1000, Winthrop, WA 98862; (509)996-2211.** Day-trips on 30 miles of groomed trails and 20 miles of ungroomed but marked trails for guests of wilderness lodge above the Methow Valley. Five-day inn-to-inn ski tours in the Methow Valley offered from January through March. Lessons and equipment rental also available. Cost: $40-60/night, includes lodging and trail use; $300 for inn-to-inn tours. (TA)

# Oregon

**Ben Banks or Margie Parks, High Wallowas, P.O. Box 128, Joseph, OR 97846; (503)432-5331.** Cross-country or ski-mountaineering trips on the backside of the High Wallowas. Ski trips begin with a gondola ride 8,200 feet up the mountain. Trips available from November to April, depending on snow. Cost: $60.

**Julia Porter or Marcia Munson, Keep Listening Wilderness Trips for Women, P.O. Box 446, Sandy, OR 97055; (503)239-6896.** Two- to 3-day ski-touring lessons near Mt. Hood from January to March. Beginning skills taught in supportive, noncompetitive atmosphere. Cost: $16-115,

depending on income.

**Bob Matthews, Mt. Bachelor Nordic Sports Center, P.O. Box 1031, Bend, OR 97701; (503)382-8334.** Twelve miles of groomed, maintained trails and 3 miles of untracked terrain in the Three Sisters Wilderness are available to cross-country skiers for a small trail-use fee. Lessons and rental equipment available. Cost: $2/day for trail use, $7 for group lessons, $14 for day-tours. (TA)

# Idaho

**Joe or Sheila Leonard, Leonard Expeditions, Box 98, Stanley, ID 83278; (208) 774-3656.** Hut-to-hut skiing in the Sawtooth Mountains for 5 to 7 days. Portable huts are equipped with wood stoves. Six-day tent and snow-cave tours also offered for experienced skiers, as well as backcountry ski clinics for all levels of ability. Cost: $185-475 for hut-to-hut trips, $350-410 for 6-day tent and snow-cave tours. (TA)

**The Tonsmeires, Wilderness River Outfitters and Trail Expeditions, Inc., P.O. Box 871, Salmon, ID 83467; (208)756-3959.** A variety of 2-, 3-, and 5-day trips beginning with a scenic flight to Salmon. Basic techniques for cross-country winter travel are taught while group skis, overnighting in prepared huts. Five-day clinics also offered, consisting of 3 days of instruction and 2 days of mountain skiing. Cost: $250 for 2-day trips, $310 for 3-day trips, $400 for 5-day trips. (TA)

# California

**Ken Hanley, Adventure Unique, 19 Washington St., Santa Clara, CA 95050;**

(408)243-4878. Weekend trips with a night in a cabin at Tahoe or camping on a meadow in the High Sierra Nevada. Each trip is designed to be a learning experience in outdoor skills and the natural environment. Also offered are a nordic ski school in December and a class in cross-country techniques in the High Sierra over the New Year's holiday. Cost: $55-65 for weekend trips, $88 for ski school, $95 for New Year's trip. (TA)

**Kirkwood Ski Touring Center, P.O. Box 77, Kirkwood, CA 95646; (209)258-8864.** Lessons, races, and 1-day and moonlight tours are among offerings during winter months. Touring center has complete maintained trail system open to public use. Cost: $2/day for trail use, $8-15 for lessons, $10 for day-tours, $5 for moonlight tours.

**Alan Ehrgott or Butch Carber, Pacific Adventures, Box 5041, Riverside, CA 92517; (714)685-1227.** Three-day trip through the backcountry of Yosemite Valley in February. Deluxe accommodations in cabins; lessons available if desired. Cost: $220. (TA)

**Palisade School of Mountaineering, P.O. Box 694, Bishop, CA 93514; (714) 935-4330.** Ski-mountaineering courses near Mammoth Lakes and guided alpine ski tours in the Sierra Nevada offered in winter. Courses include instruction in roped skiing, belaying and rappelling on skis, and snow camping. Applicants must be strong enough to ski with a pack. Cost: $435 for courses.

**Jonathan Wiesel, Royal Gorge Nordic Ski Resort, P.O. Box 178, Soda Springs, CA 95728; (916)622-3871.** Trails, ski school, and overnight guided trips available. Overnight trips feature snow camping and instruction in building snow shelters, cooking, and bivouacking. Weekend ski packages at mountain lodge that features French cuisine also offered. Cost: $45 for overnight trips, $5/day for trail use, $75/day for guide/instructor for maximum of 5 persons, $105 for weekend packages. (TA)

**Guy Peto, Sierra Nomad Ski Touring, P.O. Box 655, El Dorado, CA 95623; (916)622-2566.** Two- or 5-day snow-camping trips and 2- or 3-day resort weekend trips in the Hope Valley, Carson Pass area. Trips are of various levels of difficulty. Day-tours and ski instruction also available. Trips offered from December to April. Cost: $10 for day-tours, $40 for 2-day snow-camping trips, $60 for 2-day resort trips, $90 for 3-day trips, cost-sharing basis for 5-day trips.

**Mark Ewing, Squaw Valley Nordic Center, P.O. Box 2499, Olympic Valley, CA 95730; (916)583-4284.** Two-, 3-, and 5-day skiing trips into the Sierra Nevada near Squaw Valley during winter months. Climbing and mountain craft also taught. Cost: available upon request.

**Yosemite Mountaineering School and Guide Service, Yosemite National Park, CA 95389; (209)372-4611 ext. 244.** Wide variety of guided tours and instructional programs in Yosemite National Park. Courses range from an introduction to ski touring to touring survival, and tours include a 6-day trip in the Sierra-Tuolumne Meadows. Cost: $13 for daily instruction, $38 for 2-day tours, $55 for 3-day tours.

# DIVING

Not content to mimic birds by flying in hang gliders, people have always sought to swim like fish, too, both on the surface of the water and beneath it. For centuries, pearl divers in Polynesia have been plunging to depths of over 100 feet on no more than a breath of air. The ancients from Aristotle onward speculated on devices—from pipes to pig bladders—that would allow breathing while underwater. But it has been only in the last forty years that practical developments have given divers the flexibility and comfort necessary to enjoy the underwater world.

Although there are warm currents and inlets even in the Northwest, most people who dive here prefer wearing a wet suit because it increases the amount of time a person can safely enjoy being underwater. The suits allow a bit of water to seep in between the neoprene foam shell and the skin, where it is warmed by body heat and acts as insulation. The suits must be worn with a weight belt to offset their buoyancy. The scuba gear itself—the Self-Contained Underwater Breathing Apparatus—consists of a tank or two of compressed air, worn in a back harness, and a breathing valve that regulates air intake and allows exhalation. A face mask improves underwater vision, and flippers provide added strength to a diver's kick in the slow-moving world beneath the surface.

The warm waters, burning sun, and colorful corals of the tropics are most often associated with diving, but some of the clearest waters and most abundant marine life-forms in the world are found in the Northwest. The still waters of Puget Sound and the Strait of Georgia are an increasingly popular arena for underwater exploration, and diving outfitters and clubs are becoming ever more common. Prime diving spots can be visited on trips led by experienced divers who know the underwater world—from starfish to sunken ships. Air compressors are often included to refill scuba tanks between dives. In some cases, the scuba gear itself can be rented for the duration of the trip.

Undersea fishing is one reason people dive, but the spear gun is being replaced by the camera in much the same way as the big gun is being traded in for the telephoto lens on animal safaris. Special waterproof, pressure-resistant housings are available to fit most models of thirty-five millimeter cameras, and a few models made specifically for underwater use are on the market. Often, flash attachments are necessary to compensate for the low light at depths greater than a few feet. With practice, an ordinary diver can make surprisingly beautiful photographs of a world that, until recently, was virtually inaccessible to human view, hidden beneath the inscrutable face of the sea.

# British Columbia

**Beach Gardens Dive Resort, 7074 Westminster Ave., Powell River, B.C., Canada V8A 1C5; (604)485-6267.** Three-, 5-, and 7-night diving packages year-round at 14-acre resort, including boat- and shore-diving, in area with underwater shipwreck. Resort also offers pool, spa, and tennis courts. Cost: $185-225(Cdn.) for 3 nights, $285-355 for 5 nights, $424-527 for 7 nights. (TA)

**Gordon L. Bradley, Star Fire Charters, IBM Marine, Inc., 9119 12th Ave. N.E., Seattle, WA 98115; (206)525-9851.** One-day, weekend, or 5-day trips in Puget Sound and Canadian waters, offered from May through October. Trips are led by experienced dive masters, and the boat has a 10 CFM compressor. All diving passengers must be certified. Fishing equipment and licenses and all meals provided. Cost: available upon request. (TA)

# Washington

**Gordon L. Bradley, Star Fire Charters, IBM Marine, Inc., 9119 12th Ave. N.E., Seattle, WA 98115; (206)525-9851.** See British Columbia listing.

# FISHING

Fishing is one of the major industries of the Northwest, and fish are second only to timber in being the region's most important natural resource. This is an ancient heritage: for hundreds of years, the Indians of the coast and rivers depended on fish as their major food source, a dependence that is reflected in their mythology and art. Many of the rivers are named for the tribes that lived along them, catching salmon and trout by means of harpoons, nets, traps, and even baited hooks. Despite some depletion in salmon runs in recent years, recreational fishing still almost guarantees a backcountry meal throughout the Northwest or an exciting day of open-sea fishing in the waters of the Pacific.

Steelhead, salmon, and trout are the major recreational catches in the rivers and lakes of this region. Although steelhead can be as big as king or Chinook salmon, they are actually a subspecies of rainbow trout, which migrate to the open sea as do salmon. Catches of over thirty pounds have been recorded, while in certain areas the average is ten pounds or more. King salmon usually weigh between twenty and twenty-five pounds, though a ninety-three-pound open-sea catch is on record. The coho (or silver) salmon is next in size at five to ten pounds, followed by the smaller sockeye, pink, and chum. Dolly Varden, cutthroat, and rainbow trout are all common to Northwest inland waters, and catches of around five pounds are not unusual. Favorite fish from salt water include cod, halibut, bass, tuna, and red snapper. For even more variety, some sea-going trips include time for setting crab traps or digging for clams or oysters along tidal beaches.

On commercial pleasure-fishing trips, guides take you to the best angling spots—perhaps a quiet hole beneath rapids on a Cascades river, a mountain lake in the Purcells that is accessible only by several days of backpacking, or a rocky sub-marine ridge off the Oregon coast. On some trips fishing equipment, including bait and hooks, is provided, while on others just the boat charter and the captain's knowledge of waters and currents are included.

A good angler follows the seasons, knows when the salmon begin running and trout reach maturity, and knows, too, the legal limits of catches. It is possible to "fish out" a stream or area, and for some species such overharvesting never can be overcome. Limits are put not only on the number of fish that may be taken but also on their size so as not to deplete a healthy breeding stock. Know the local limits and be sure your guide knows them, too. Despite the pleasures that can be derived from wading knee deep in a gurgling mountain stream, the responsibility of the fisherman to his sport must not be overlooked.

# British Columbia

Ron From, Alpine Wilderness Retreat, 11744 80th Ave., Delta, B.C., Canada V4C 1X9; (604)596-9334. Guided fishing trips to 8 small lakes accessible by hiking, canoeing, and portaging, offered between June 1 and September 30. Trips can be tailored to specific groups' desires; no more than 20 persons to a group. Cost: $60(Cdn.)/day.

Ken High or Vern Horton, Babine River Steelhead Lodge, Ltd., 601 W. Spruce, Missoula, MT 59801; (406)543-6056. Sun-up to sundown fishing for a week on the river acclaimed as the world's best steel-head-fishing waters, from September to mid-November. Only 1 steelhead may be kept for mounting—all others are released. Coho salmon and cutthroat and Dolly Varden trout are also plentiful and may be kept; they will be smoked or frozen at no charge. Rustic lodge has a wilderness setting. Cost: $695(U.S.).

Terry or June Benesh, Bare Lake Resort, P.O. Box 559, Peachland, B.C., Canada V0H 1X0; (604)767-3462 or 768-7444, or 100 Mile House radio 93759, JS channel. Fishing for Kamloops trout, which range from 1 to 6 pounds, on 6 remote lakes in pine- and meadow-covered wilderness area. Hunting trips also available. Lodge is accessible only by air and open from June 1 to September 30. Two-day minimum stay. Cost: $60/day.

Buzz Kyllonen, Barkley-Nahmint Fishing Lodge, 8303 Juanita Dr. N.E., Seattle, WA 98155; (206)823-9696. Four-day, 3-night packages for king and silver salmon fishing offered in August and September. Wilderness lodge accessible only by air. Fishing techniques seminars are offered, so guides, though available, are not required. Beachcombing, canoeing, visiting the nearby fishing village of Bamfield, and observing wildlife are other popular activities. Unlimited use of boat for fishing and exploring. Cost: $650, includes air transportation from Seattle.

Brian McDonald, Black Tusk Touring and Guide Service Ltd., 3064 St. Kildas Ave., N. Vancouver, B.C., Canada V7N 2A9; (604)985-9223. Two-week fishing trips from May through October, including 4 days in Campbell River, known for excellent salmon fishing, and a week at Babine Lake, which has rainbow, lake, and Dolly Varden trout, coho salmon, and whitefish in summer, and steelhead averaging 14 pounds in fall. Guides will give instruction in fishing techniques if desired. Air transportation provided from Vancouver; lodging in Vancouver included in package. Cost: $1,595 from May through August, $1,705 in September and October.

Harold Lacy or Bruce Grant, Gilbert's Marine & Guide Service Ltd., 789 Saunders Lane, Brentwood Bay, B.C., Canada V0S 1A0; (604)652-2211. Year-round salmon fishing from fully-equipped cabin boats with professional guides. Bass, lingcod, red snapper, and rock fish also may be taken. Cost: available upon request.

Tom Land or Kathy Moore, Good Hope Cannery Lodge, P.O. Box 4244, Bellevue, WA 98009; (206)623-4894. Guided salmon fishing on Rivers Inlet, British Columbia, known for trophy runs of Chinook and coho salmon, from luxurious lodge that features high level of service and gourmet food. Three-, 4-, and 7-day packages available from June 1 to September 30. Fishing gear is provided. Fly-in fishing to area lakes can be arranged. Hiking, crabbing, clamming, and scenic and historical tours also available. Cost: $900(Cdn.) and up, includes air transportation from Vancouver, B.C. (TA)

The Rathbuns, Headwaters Fishing Camp, Box 350, Peachland, B.C., Canada V0H 1X0; Vernon radio YP9-4825, JP channel. Year-round fishing for rainbow and brook trout on Headwaters Lakes, which are restocked each year. Camp has scenic mountain setting and offers housekeeping cabins, campgrounds, and coffee shop. Cost: available upon request.

**Peter L. Gordon, Magna Charters Ltd.,
902 Deal St., Victoria, B.C., Canada V8S
5G3; (602)598-4213.** Year-round guided
salmon fishing from cabin boat in Pedder
Bay/Church Rock area near Victoria.
Specialty is helping the novice. Orcas,
otters, and bald eagles often observed.
Cost: $44/half-day, includes tackle, bait,
and coffee. (TA)

**Kaare Halvorsen, Pacific Viking Fishing
Resort, Kon Tiki Island, Kyuquot, B.C.,
Canada V0P 1J0.** Salmon fishing and
clamming on a 7-acre private island off
the west coast of Vancouver Island, open
year-round. Cod, halibut, mussels, and
crab also are abundant, as are trout in a
nearby river. Possible activities also include swimming, hiking, and beachcombing. Rooms have shared cooking and
housekeeping facilities. Cost: $59/week,
double occupancy, May 1 through October 1; lower off-season rates.

**H. Cody Tegart, Palliser River Guides and
Outfitters Inc., Brisco, B.C., Canada V0A
1B0; (604)346-3260.** Horsepacking into secluded areas of the Royal Group of mountains for cutthroat trout fishing and sight-
seeing, July 15 to September 5. Mountain
camp of chalets and tents. Minimum
3-day trip. Cost: $85-95 for 3 days,
depending on number in party.

**Rivers Inlet Resort, 3204 N.E. 123rd, P.O.
Box 25714, Seattle, WA 98125; (206)
365-0616.** Four-day, 3-night trip to secluded fjord on the coast of British Columbia, accessible only by air, for king
and coho salmon fishing. Crabbing, clamming, halibut and cod fishing also available, and wildlife is often observed. Unlimited and exclusive use of a boat; guides
available at extra charge. Open June 1 to
September 5. Cost: $750-1,000, depending
on accommodations desired and month,
includes air transportation from Seattle.
(TA)

**Lioel Thompson, Shangri-la Wilderness
Camp, Spillimacheen, B.C., Canada V0A
1P0; (604)346-3217.** Remote wilderness
camp in an alpine basin of the Purcell
Mountains, accessible only by helicopter,

offers fishing at 10 mountain lakes for
rainbow and cutthroat trout, and stream
fishing as well. Camp consists of 6-foot
tents with plywood floors, wood heaters,
and gas lighting. Glaciers and 10,000-foot
peaks make this area excellent for photographers. Cost: $150/person/day for 3-6
persons, $125/person/day for 7-15 per-
sons, $100/person/day for 16-20 persons,
includes meals, guides, and round-trip
helicopter transportation from Spillimacheen.

**Gordon L. Bradley, Star Fire Charters,
IBM Marine, Inc., 9119 12th Ave. N.E.,
Seattle, WA 98115; (206)525-9851.** Ocean-
running boat offers 1-day trips around
Puget Sound, weekend trips to San Juan

Islands, and 5-day excursions into Canadian waters, year-round. Boat carries 6 small catch boats with motors, and all fishing gear. Homecooked gourmet food is served. Trips are tailored to guests' desires. Cost: $30 for 1-day trips. (TA)

Jim or Myrna Boulding, Strathcona Park Lodge and Outdoor Education Centre, Box 2160, Campbell River, B.C., Canada V9W 5C9; Campbell River radio, Strathcona Lodge 59 7021. Six-day fishing methods courses in summer in area famous for trout, cod, and salmon. Instruction includes how to fish with flies, troll, use a bucktail, and set a crab trap. Overnight camping may be required. Cost: $245(Cdn.). (TA)

Bob or Linda Waknuk, Ta-Weel Lake Fishing Lodge, Little Fort, B.C., Canada V0E 2C0; (604)677-4373 or Barriere, B.C., mobile operator, radio phone YL 96050. Minimum of 4 days fishing for Kamloops trout on lake at 4,000-feet elevation. Boats are provided, and fish are cleaned, and ice-packed or smoked at no charge. Rustic cabins in variety of sizes; homecooked meals provided. Cost: $42/day, includes jeep service from Kamloops.

Bernie or Swede Gano, Tee Slash Dee Ranch, Anahim Lake, B.C., Canada V0L 1C0; Williams Lake radio, Chilanko channel, 8-L71. Custom fishing trips for small groups from wilderness working ranch. Cost: $75-80/day.

# Washington

Stu Thornton, Dogfish Charters, 1528 Evergreen Pl., Tacoma, WA 98466; (206) 564-6609. Year-round bottom fishing on Puget Sound, leaving daily from Port Townsend and Tacoma. Ninety percent of passengers catch limit. Some boats modified to handle wheelchair patients. Equipment provided; passengers provide own meals. Cost: $25-30.

Terry Manthey, The King Connection, 119 140th St. S.E., Everett, WA 98204; (206)745-0262. One-day fly-fishing trips for steelhead and sea-run cutthroat trout in September and October, winter-run steelhead from November through March. Party limit of 2 persons. Passengers provide own meals. Cost: $125 for 2 persons.

Jeff Utz, Outdoor Adventures, Box 500, Gold Bar, WA 98251; (206)282-8887 or 793-1166. One-day or overnight freshwater fishing trips to out-of-the-way places with instruction provided. Fishing license and equipment required. Cost: $25 for day-trips; $68 for overnight, includes 3 meals.

David Button, Pacific Northwest Float Trips, 829 Waldron St., Sedro Woolley, WA 98284; (206)855-0535. Year-round day-trips on the Skagit and Nooksack rivers to fish for steelhead, rainbow and Dolly Varden trout, and king salmon (depending on season). Cost $35.

Les Adams, Puget Sound Fishing Charters, 1209 Monroe Ave. N.E., Renton, WA 98055; (206)255-1936. Daily salmon-fishing trips from Seattle on calm waters in Puget Sound offered year-round. Boat is Martin Tackle Company's research vessel and thus has latest tackle equipment and offers tackle instruction. It also is equipped with electronic fish-finders. Fish are cleaned and wrapped at no charge; passengers provide own meals. Bottom-fishing trips can be arranged. Cost: available upon request.

Gordon L. Bradley, Star Fire Charters, IBM Marine, Inc., 9119 12th Ave. N.E., Seattle, WA 98115; (206)525-9851. See British Columbia listing.

Ken McDonald, Viking Star Charters, 3629 Bagley N., Seattle, WA 98103; (206)634-2939. Daily skippered charter fishing in Puget Sound for salmon and bottom fish, offered year-round. Boat has electronic fish-finding equipment. Special charters, including overnight cruises, can be arranged. Cost: $35; $4 for tackle rental. (TA)

# Oregon

**Ray Baker, Ray Baker's White Water Guide Service, 88664 Faulhaber Rd., Elmira, OR 97437; (503)935-3688.** Year-round fishing trips of varying length on Oregon rivers and coastal streams. Three and 4-day trips on white-water rivers to fish for steelhead and rainbow trout offered May through August. Fishing techniques taught. Cost: $125/day. (TA)

**Wayne Gardner, Wayne Gardner Guide and Outfitter, Greenwood Dr., Leaburg, OR 97401; (503)896-3615 or 3215.** Three-day lodge trips on the Rogue River in fall. Other fishing trips on Oregon rivers offered year-round. Cost: $25-400. (TA)

**Dave Helfrich River Outfitter, Inc., 47555 McKenzie Hwy., Vida, OR 97488; (503) 896-3786.** Day-trips offered from late April to October to fly-fish for trout in the McKenzie River from McKenzie River drift boats. Cost: $100/boat (1 or 2 persons).

**Jerry Hughes or Carole Finley, Hughes River Expeditions, Inc., P.O. Box 217, Cambridge, ID 83610; (208)257-3477.** River-rafting company offers some special fishing trips on eastern Oregon rivers in spring, summer, and fall. Cost: available upon request.

**Galand Hass, Northwest Whitewater Excursions, P.O. Box 10754, Eugene, OR 97440; (503)266-2974.** A variety of fishing trips in drift boats on Oregon rivers and coast offered year-round. Camp equipment and furniture are provided and meals feature gourmet outdoor cooking. Cost: $130/boat for 1-day trips to $500/person for 4-day trips. (TA)

**Gene or Ted Owens, Gene and Ted Owens Fishing Guide Service, 11805 S.E.** 56th Ave., Milwaukie, OR 97222; (503) 659-1643 or 761-5358. Steelhead, salmon, and trout fishing from drift boats or jet-sleds on Clackamas, Sandy, and Molalla rivers, December through June, and on Deschutes River, July through October. White water is covered, and scenic country offers good photographic opportunities. Minimum of 3 days required for drift-boat trips. Guides are Red Cross certified. Cost: $250/day/jet-sled with up to 4 persons per boat, $220/day/drift boat with up to 2 persons per boat, on the Deschutes; $140/day/jet-sled with up to 3 persons per boat, $90/day/drift boat with up to 2 persons per boat, on other rivers.

**Gary Rhinehart, Rhinehart's Guide Service, 5649 McLoughlin Dr., Central Point, OR 97502; (503)779-1880.** White-water fishing trips on the Rogue and Deschutes rivers, May through November. Deluxe camping with fine food. Good photographic opportunities. Cost: $230 for 3-day trips, $280 for 4-day trips.

**Irv Urie, River Trips Unlimited, 900 Murphy Rd., Medford, OR 97501; (503) 779-3798.** Summer-run steelhead fly-fishing trips through the wild section of the Rogue River, August 20 through November 20. Lodging, breakfast, and dinner during 4-day trips are provided in rustic lodges along the river. Cost: $525. (TA)

**Ken Robertson & Sons Guide Service, 3424 Amber Lane, Grants Pass, OR 97526; (503)479-9554.** Four-day guided steelhead-fishing trips in drift boats on the Rogue River, with rustic lodge accommodations. Trips are offered September 8 through November 15. Cost: $425.

**Rogue River Outfitters, 8890 Rogue River Hwy., P.O. Box 618, Rogue River, OR 97537; (503)582-3101.** Salmon- and steelhead-fishing trips in jet boats or drift boats on the Rogue River. Equipment provided. Custom-planned trips and multi-day camp and lodge trips also available. Cost: $35-45 for ½-day trips, $60-85 for 1-day trips.

**Larry Bigbee, Sportcraft Marina, 1701**

Clackamette Dr., Oregon City, OR 97045; (503)656-6484. Guided fishing trips on Oregon rivers tailored to needs and desires of group. Cost: available upon request.

Michael R. Saul, Sundance Expeditions Inc., 14894 Galice Rd., Merlin, OR 97532; (503)479-8508. Three-day, 2-night steelhead-fishing trips in the fall and ½-day or 1-day salmon-fishing trips in the spring, on the Rogue River. Lodge accommodations. Custom trips also available. Cost: $325 for 3-day trips, $75/boat (1 or 2 persons) for ½-day trips, $125/boat for 1-day trips.

Mike Carey, Whitewater Guide Trips, Inc., 12120 S.W. Douglas, Portland, OR 97225; (503)646-8849. Fishing trips in McKenzie River boats for winter steelhead, spring and fall Chinook salmon, and cutthroat trout, September through June. Two-to-one guest-to-guide ratio. Cost: $150/day for 2 persons.

# Idaho

Harold Thomas, Allison Ranch, 5727 Hill Rd., Boise, ID 83703; (208)344-0951. Spring and fall steelhead fishing from wilderness ranch near some of the best fishing holes on the Salmon River. Possible activities also include horseback riding, hiking, swimming, and hunting. Ranch is accessible only by air and available on a weekly basis to only 1 party, with a maximum of 8 persons, at a time. Cost: $285.

Jerry Hughes or Carole Finley, Hughes River Expeditions, Inc., P.O. Box 217, Cambridge, ID 83610; (208)257-3477. See Oregon listing.

Bob Volpert, Outdoor Adventures Inc., 3109 Fillmore St., San Francisco, CA 94123; (415)346-8700. Six-day trips in September on the Middle Fork of the Salmon River for fly-fishing instruction from a recognized expert. Both basic skills and advanced techniques taught. Limited to 12 persons. Cost: $935. (TA)

Stephen Dixon, Salmon River Lodge, Inc., P.O. Box 348, Jerome, ID 83338; (208)324-3553 or 5568. One-day steelhead fishing from jet boats on Salmon River in February, March, October, and November. Cost: $55. (TA)

Bob or Jan Sevy, Sevy Guide Service, P.O. Box 1527, Sun Valley, ID 83353; (208)788-3440. Custom-tailored trips on Idaho rivers for small groups. Overnight trips are camping trips with a campfire each evening; highlight of each trip is fish feed. Cost: available upon request.

Bill Mason, The Snug Co., Box 598, Sun Valley, ID 83353; (208)622-9305. Guides direct fishermen to appropriate water in and around Sun Valley, where cutthroat, rainbow, brook, and brown trout are plentiful, and provide instruction in all aspects of fly-fishing techniques. Limit of two persons per guide. Half-day on-site fly-fishing school also available, as well as specific-technique seminars for instruction in precise areas of the sport. Cost: $125 for 2 persons for 1 day of guide service, includes lunch and transportation; $50 for half-day school.

# California

Bill or Lela Claypole, Beaver Creek Lodge, Klamath River, CA 96050; (916) 465-2246. Guided steelhead fishing, September through March. Equipment and lunch provided. Freezing and smoking service available. Cost: $110-120/day/boat (1 or 2 persons).

Brad Jackson or Mike Michalak, The Fly Shop, 2727 Churn Creek Rd., Redding, CA 96001; (916)246-9988. Guided 1- or 2-day fly-fishing trips emphasizing instruction in entomology and casting techniques. Cost: available upon request.

**Chuck Stranahan, Hat Creek Anglers, P.O. Box 236, Burney, CA 96013; (916) 335-3165.** Half-day and 1-day trips to fly-fish for trout, tailored to guests' desires. Geological diversity provides wide variety of water types and fishing conditions, and trips often include 2 bodies of water in a day. Cost: available upon request.

**Alvin or Juanita Larson, Klamath Jet Boats, Inc., P.O. Box 129, Klamath, CA 95548; (707)482-4191.** Guided steelhead-fishing trips arranged. Cost: available upon request.

**Irv Urie, River Trips Unlimited, 900 Murphy Rd., Medford, OR 97501; (503)779-3798.** See Oregon listing.

**Jeff or Brad Throgmorton, Somes Bar Guide Service, Somes Bar, CA 95568; (916)469-3399.** Guided steelhead fishing daily from late August to April on Klamath River. McKenzie River drift boats used; remote pools, white water, and shaded deep-canyon pools fished each day. Equipment provided. Cost: $50/day.

# HANG GLIDING

To take part in many of the Northwest's adventures, you need to be in good physical condition and be curious about the experience, the wildlife, or scenery. The guide usually does the rest, pointing out features of interest, explaining the basic skills, and helping you out of the tight spots. Hang gliding is different. Once you learn the techniques of flying these lightweight, nylon and aluminum wings, you are pretty much on your own. Whether you skim just a couple of feet above the ground or soar hundreds of feet high on rising currents of air, the sense of flight is the same. You are as close to the ancient dream of flying like the birds as it is now possible for humans to come.

For many, the altitude and release from gravity are intimidating. For a few, they are intoxicating, and it is for them that the sport of hang gliding exists. From a running start down a grassy slope or a daring leap off a cliff, you are borne into the sky by the wind. As pilot and sole passenger, you hang from a harness below the broad wings of the glider; you control the flight by moving a bar, and make turns by shifting your weight. With practice and knowledge of wind currents, you can increase your time in the air or the distance over which you fly.

Although hang gliding may seem to be a dangerous sport, as it certainly can be, the statistics show that it is no more dangerous than any other type of flying. This is partly due to the emphasis on safety in all hang-gliding courses. Over the several hours of training, novices learn to anticipate the wind, control their gliders, and steer clear of obstacles. Nearly all areas where the sport is heavily practiced are in the open, away from the trees and telephone and power lines that are the sport's greatest hazards.

It's a good idea to make sure your instructor is certified by the United States Hang Gliding Association, a nonprofit organization that also certifies records, issues flying ratings, charters hang-gliding clubs, and otherwise promotes the sport. Proper training, good equipment, and a positive attitude are essential to enjoyable, safe hang gliding. As you enter the USHGA's pilot proficiency program, in which you must prove your ability to fly in circumstances of increasing difficulty, you'll find that you can soar farther and higher than you ever imagined.

# British Columbia

Larry Croome, Canadian Ultralight Soaring School, Box 640, Lumby, B.C., Canada V0E 2G0; (604)547-6413. Four-, 6-, and 10-day courses in hang gliding offered year-round. Ten-day course includes introduction to mountain flying. Cost: $140-290.

# California

Chandelle San Francisco, 198 Los Banos Ave., Daly City, CA 94014; (415)756-0650. Free introductory ground school, a prerequisite to taking basic lessons, is offered every Friday night year-round. Lesson packages include 2 lessons with 1 ground school and 5 lessons with 5 ground schools. Advanced lessons and organized weekend trips also offered. Cost: $99 for 2-lesson package, $225 for 5-lesson package.

Hang Gliders West, 20-A Pamaron Way, Ignazio, CA 94947; (415)883-3494. Lessons offered year-round using radio-equipped gliders. Equipment rental and repair also available. Cost: $40/lesson, $100 for 3-lesson package.

Mission Soaring Center, 43551 Mission Blvd., Fremont, CA 94538; (415)656-6656. Year-round courses offered using many different training sites. Basic flight course includes 5 flying days and 5 ground schools; introductory course includes 2 flying days and 2 ground schools. Advanced lessons also available. Cost: $215 for 5-lesson package, $105 for 2-lesson package.

# HELI-SKIING

Heli-skiing is not really an outdoor sport at all, or even a specific activity. But it is a unique combination of endeavors that makes an exhilarating adventure. Mountain skiing offers virgin snow in remote valleys, far different from the long lines and packed slopes found at the crowded ski areas. Helicopter or, in some cases, small-plane flights over the jagged ridges and smooth white basins of the interior provide views unparalleled in their grandeur. United, mountain skiing and helicopter lifts create scenic and stimulating experiences in the backcountry, where your finest skills are put to the test.

Heli-skiing is a sport for experts, or those who are at least competent and confident. The aerial flights take you miles into the wilderness, where snow conditions range from the very best anywhere to the worst. Sudden inclement weather cannot easily be avoided at isolated ski areas where there is no lodge. Avalanches are a real hazard in uncontrolled downhill areas. Even for the expert skier, the occasional broken leg or twisted knee is a possibility. But these disadvantages are more than compensated for by the direct contact with a wild skiing environment—the long downhill runs, the unmarked and mogul-free slopes, and the intoxicating atmosphere of high-altitude sport enjoyed with a few like-minded companions.

Experience counts in a sport as intense as heli-skiing, and experience also has proven some types of equipment better suited than others for this deep-powder skiing. Short, soft skis are preferred, and poles without straps are best for easy discard in case of avalanche. Good boots, gloves, goggles, and bindings are equally important. All guides are well equipped with first-aid and safety equipment, and in most cases skiers are required to wear small radio transmitters to facilitate a possible avalanche rescue.

British Columbia is the locale for the bulk of Northwest heli-skiing trips because it has the largest tracts of undeveloped mountains. In the Coast Mountains, the most heavily glaciated range in North America, helicopters fly from Whistler to snowfields near and far. In southeastern British Columbia, trips are available to such subranges of the Rockies as the Cariboos, Monashees, and Bugaboos, offering some of the most impressive isolated skiing in the world. Or you can be flown to the Assiniboine Lodge, instead of skiing over thirty-five difficult miles to get there. Wherever you end up, once the engines are shut off you're alone with your skis and skills in the wilderness.

# British Columbia

Ron Banner, Air Alps Ltd., Box 2014, Squamish, B.C., Canada V0N 3G0; (604) 898-9016. Guided glacier skiing in the Misty Ice Fields, with 10,000 vertical feet of powder skiing, offered from onset of winter to approximately April 30. Ski-plane transportation into the Coast Range ice fields also available for ski mountaineering parties. Cost: $90 and up for guided ski trips, $180-200 per hour of air time for other trips. (TA)

Herb Bleuer, B.C. Powder Guides, P.O. Box 258, Whistler, B.C., Canada V0N 1B0; (604)932-5331 or 894-6994. Daily heli-skiing tours from December 15 to May 15 from Whistler, including 12,000 vertical feet of helicopter lift and 3 runs on 3 different glaciers. Three-day packages from Bralorne, including lodging, meals, and 40,000 vertical feet of helicopter lift, offered from late February through early March. Seven-day packages in a very remote area of the Coast Range with excellent powder snow, including hunting lodge accommodations and meals and 100,000 vertical feet of helicopter lift, offered in March from Taseko. Cost: $140(Cdn.) for 1-day tours, $600 for 3-day packages, $1,590 for 7-day packages. (TA)

Canadian Mountain Holidays Ltd., P.O. Box 1660, Banff, Alta., Canada T0L 0C0; (403)762-4531. Daily heli-skiing trips from Radium for skiing south of the Bugaboos and from Valemount for skiing in the Cariboos, including 3,000 meters of helicopter lift, guide, avalanche radio, and lunch. Five- and 7-day packages from Radium and Valemount also available, as well as 7-day packages from Revelstoke, all featuring in-town accommodations. Seven-day packages at Bobbie Burns, the Monashees, the Cariboos, and the Bugaboos offered with accommodations at base-camp lodges. All overnight packages include lodging, meals, guide service, and helicopter lift, and most include round-trip transportation from Calgary or Edmonton. Season is from late December through early May. Cost: $950-1,180 (Cdn.) for 5-day packages, $1,000-1,980 for 7-day packages. (TA)

Mike Wiegele, Cariboo Helicopter Skiing Ltd., P.O. Box 1824, Banff, Alta., Canada T0L 0C0; (403)762-4171. Seven-day ski packages based in Blue River, British Columbia, offered from mid-January to early May. Includes bus transportation from Kamloops, British Columbia, double-occupancy accommodations, meals, daily helicopter lift, and guide. Cost: $1,365(Cdn.) in high season (late January to early April), $1,280 in low season. (TA)

Jonathan Wiesel, Royal Gorge Nordic Ski Resort, Inc., P.O. Box 178, Soda Springs, CA 95728; (916)426-3871. One 7-day trip in mid-April to Mt. Assiniboine, known as the Matterhorn of Canada. Lodging and meals that feature French provincial cuisine provided at rustic, remote chalet at 7,100-feet elevation. Cost: $500 from Calgary. (TA)

# HORSEPACKING

The Hollywood western has sparked in most of us a longing for wide-open spaces, rugged canyons, and the honest companionship of a horse. Such desires need not be fulfilled through only movies and dreams, for the Northwest has a number of outfitters who supply all the horses, equipment, and training necessary to ride the high country. From the uninhabited tundra of northernmost British Columbia to the trout-filled streams of the High Sierra Nevada, from the alpine lakes of the North Cascades to the pristine granite mountains of the Sawtooth Wilderness, horsepacking trips take you not only into the backcountry but also into the legacy of North America.

Although a few of these adventures call for experienced riders, most of them are suitable for the novice who has never been on horseback. All that is required is generally good physical condition, a positive attitude toward animals, and a willingness to step a bit off the beaten path. The animals usually are well trained and tolerant but not so haltered that they won't want to gallop down the trail at the sheer pleasure of being in the backwoods. Trips can range from a half-day ride around a crater lake in Oregon's Central Cascades to two-week pack trips in the Spatsizi Wilderness of British Columbia. Accordingly, the equipment you will need may vary considerably, but smooth-soled boots, a hat for rain and sun,

and tough clothing to withstand the rigors of the trail are essential. You may want to add fishing gear or camera equipment to this, even for the briefest of trips.

There are several basic types of horsepacking trips, designed for the wide range of outdoor experiences people like to pursue. *Horsepack trips* are those in which a horse carries your gear, food, and other supplies while you hike to your destination. *Horseback trips* are those in which a horse carries both you and your gear, with other horses carrying excess cargo. *Spot-pack and dunnage trips* are for hikers or fishermen who want to spend some time in the wilderness alone. Guides and horses pack your gear in and then leave, returning to meet you at a prearranged time and place. The difference is that on spot-pack trips the guide leads you to your destination, whereas on dunnage trips you hike on your own to the site where you have instructed the guide to leave your gear. There also are *horsepacking schools* that introduce you to the skills necessary to travel safely and comfortably in the mountains with riding and pack stock. Haltering, saddling, leading, shoeing, packing, and other techniques are taught on the trail, in the enjoyable learning conditions the wilderness offers by experienced and patient guides. Having a horse to carry the load on all these trips means that the food on the trail usually is better than regular camp fare—an added incentive for many.

While most of these packing trips use horses, a few use burros because of their surefootedness and intelligence, and some even use llamas. For thousands of years, these natives of South America have been used for packing in the Andes, and their gentle disposition, agility, and curiosity add as much to a packing trip as their cargo-carrying ability. But whether you're going by horse or llama, to the foothills of the Rockies or to the Pacific coast, horsepacking is a unique and satisfying way to see the Northwest.

# British Columbia

Larry Erickson, The Alpine Outfitters, Manson Creek, B.C., Canada V0J 2H0. Eight-, 10-, and 18-day wilderness horseback trips in the uninhabited, northern high country of British Columbia offered in July and August. Abundant opportunities for wildlife observation. Horseback experience preferred but not mandatory. Cost: $1,240 for 8-day trips, $1,550 for 10-day trips, $2,360 for 18-day trips.

Brian McDonald, Black Tusk Touring and Guide Service Ltd., 3064 St. Kildas Ave., N. Vancouver, B.C., Canada V7N 2A9; (604)985-9223. Six- and 7-day horseback trips to Mt. Assiniboine with accommodations at rustic log lodges; the lodge at Mt. Assiniboine is one of the most remote in Canada. Six-day full-circle trips into the Cascade Valley with stays at 3 base camps. All trips offered July through September. Cost: $400 for 6-day Assiniboine trips, $450 for 7-day trips, $360 for full-circle trips, in July and August; $360 for 6-day Assiniboine trips, $405 for 7-day trips, $330 for full-circle trips, in September.

H. Cody Tegart, Palliser River Guides and Outfitters Inc., Brisco, B.C., Canada V0A 1B0; (604)346-3260. Horseback trips into the Royal Group of mountains for fishing, hunting, and sight-seeing. Offered from July through November for a minimum of 3 days. Cost: $255 and up.

Bernie or Swede Gano, Tee Slash Dee Ranch, Anahim Lake, B.C., Canada V0L 1C0; Williams Lake radio, Chilanko channel, 8-L71. Custom horseback trips for small groups from wilderness working ranch. Cost: $75-80/day.

# Washington

Ray or Esther Courtney, Cascade Corrals, Stehekin, WA 98852. Three- to 9-day horseback and horsepack trips in the North Cascades wilderness offered from

July through September. Requires only good health. Round-trip transportation from Chelan, Washington, provided. Two-week course on horsepacking and mountain travel with horses also offered. Cost: $130-455 for trips, $500 for course. (TA)

**Jeff Utz, Outdoor Adventures, Box 500, Gold Bar, WA 98251; (206)282-8887 or 793-1166.** Weekend and 5-day horseback trips in July and August into the Glacier Peaks and Alpine Lakes wilderness areas in the High Cascades. Inexperienced riders are welcome; time available for side trips, exploration, and fishing at lakeside campsites. Cost: $168 for weekend trips, $398 for 5-day trips.

# Oregon

**Blue Lake Resort, Star Rt., Sisters, OR 97759; (503)595-6671.** Guided horseback and horsepack trips in Sisters and Mount Jefferson wilderness areas for guests at resort. Located in Deschutes National Forest at 3,500-feet elevation, the resort is beside a volcanic-crater lake. Cost: $20-28/day for lodging for 2 persons, $6/day for travel-trailer space for 2 persons, $3/day for camp space for 2 persons.

**Flying M Ranch, Rt. 1, Box 95C, Yamhill, OR 97148; (503)662-3222.** Two- and 4-day trail rides to the ocean, Indian Heaven country, and rustic camp in the Coast Range offered in July and August. Custom rides also available for a minimum of 2 days, 15 riders. Cost: $98-230 for scheduled rides, $49/day for custom rides.

**Doris Zanelli, Hells Canyon Navigation Co., P.O. Box 145, Oxbow, OR 97840; (503)785-3352.** Six-day combination raft/horseback trips through Hells Canyon and the Wallowa Mountains in summer. Opportunity for fishing and exploring Indian and historic sites. Trips begin at Oxbow and end at Joseph, Oregon. Cost:

$429. (TA)

**Jan Henderson or Stew Morton, Lute Jerstad Adventures, P.O. Box 19527, Portland, OR 97219; (503)244-4364.** Horseback trips of any length from mid-July through September for a maximum of 12 persons. Remote trails once were hunting grounds of the Nez Perce Indians; participants can fish for trout in wilderness lakes, or spot herds of elk and deer. Combination float/horseback trips also can be arranged. Cost: available upon request. (TA)

**Jan Euhus, Red's Wallowa Horse Ranch, P.O. Box 508, Enterprise, OR 97828; (503)426-4078 or 3167.** Horses for trail riding available to guests of ranch in Eagle Cap Wilderness Area. Custom horseback or horsepack trips can be arranged in summer. Air flight or 8-mile horseback trip are only access to ranch; cost of transportation not included in daily rate. Cost: $60/day.

**Ken Warren, Ken Warren Outdoors, 9100 S.W. 92nd, Portland, OR 97266; (503) 777-1828 or 254-3245 or 638-4327.** Five-day horseback trips to the highest pass in the Wallowa Mountains, and the Eagle Cap Wilderness Area, with good opportunity for fishing and hiking. Six-day combination float/horseback trips on the Grande Ronde River and into the rugged and remote Wenaha River country; opportunity for wildlife observation and trout fishing. Eight-day combination white-water-float/horseback trips in Hells Canyon of the Snake River featuring spectacular trail vantages directly into Hells Canyon. Cost: $595 for 6-day trips, $795 for 8-day trips. (TA)

**Don Hinton, Wilderness Pack Trips, P.O. Box 71, Rogue River, OR 97537.** Three- to 5-day horseback trips offered from May through November and 5-day horsepack trips offered from April through December, through alpine forests and meadows. Spot-pack trips, for experienced campers only, can be arranged. Cost: $40/day for horseback trips, $30/day for horsepack trips, $20/day for spot-pack trips. (TA)

# Idaho

Ted, Karen, or Dan Epley, Elk Creek Ranch, Box 987, McCall, ID 98338; (208) 634-5173. Guided summer horseback trips custom tailored for parties of 2 to 8 persons. Spot-pack trips offered with maximum pack-in time of 1 day. Cost: $40 for 1-day rides, includes lunch; $50/day for overnight trips, includes camp gear and food; $60/person and $20/pack-animal for spot-pack trips.

Joan Kuebler, Mackay Bar Corporation, 3190 Airport Way, Boise, ID 83705; (208)344-1881. Four- and 6-day combination white-water-raft/horseback trips in the Main Salmon River area offered from July through mid-September. Trips include 1 to 2 days at rustic ranch, which offers fishing, hiking, and horseback riding. Cost: $565 for 4-day trips, $815 for 6-day trips, includes round-trip transportation from Boise. (TA)

Jeff Bitton, Mystic Saddle Ranch, Box 461-NA, Mountain Home, ID 83647; (208)587-5091. Three- and 7-day horseback trips in the Sawtooth Wilderness Area offered from mid-July through mid-October. Seven-day trips include 3 days at Edna Lake base camp, from which guests can ride to other lakes, climb nearby mountains, fish, read, swim or photograph. Guides teach fishing techniques if desired. Spot-pack and custom horsepack trips also available. Cost: $400 for 7-day trips, $150 for 3-day trips, $40/guide/day and $20/horse/day for spot-pack trips, $45/day for custom horsepack trips.

Archie George, Red River Corrals, Elk City, ID 93525; (208)842-2228. Horseback and horsepack trips in Selway-Bitterroot and River of No Return wilderness areas offered from June through August. Opportunity for fishing and photography. Cost: $250/week.

Stephen Dixon, Salmon River Lodge, Inc., P.O. Box 348, Jerome, ID 83338; (208)324-3553. Five- to 11-day summer horseback trips in wilderness area offering old Indian paintings and opportunity for fishing in high mountain lakes and photography. Ten-day combination float/ horseback trips also available. Cost: $450 and up for horseback trips, $850 for combination trips. (TA)

# California

Kay DeVoto, Cherry Valley Pack Station, P.O. Box 1339, Sonora, CA 95370; (209) 532-2961 in winter, or Stockton operator, Cherry Valley 2 in summer. Custom horseback, horsepack, spot-pack, and dunnage trips in the Emigrant and Yosemite wilderness areas offered from June 15 through November 1. Group trips for a minimum of 8 persons and 4 days are available, as are youth trips for children 8-years-old and up, lasting about 4 days. Burros can be rented for hikers who want a pack animal but do not require a guide. Cost: $50/guide/day, $18/pack-animal/day.

Jack Layton, Elk Creek Pack Station, Box 868, Happy Camp, CA 96039; (916)493-5421. Custom horseback, horsepack, and spot-pack trips in Marble Mountain Wilderness Area offered from June 15 through October 15. Cost: $60/guide/day, $25/pack-animal/day.

Guy Peto, Mama's Llamas, Inc., P.O. Box 655, El Dorado, CA 95623; (916)622-2566. Two- to 6-day summer hiking trips using llamas as pack animals. Trips encompass forest, wilderness, and beach areas in northern California. Participants help in all aspects of trip. Opportunity for fishing, photography, and nature study. Custom trips can be arranged for groups of 6 to 10 persons. Cost: $40-50/day.

Craig or Herbert London, Rock Creek Pack Station, Box 248, Bishop, CA 93514; (714)872-8331 in winter, (714)935-4493 in

**summer.** Custom summer horseback, horsepack, spot-pack, and dunnage trips, and 4- to 11-day scheduled horseback trips, including one 4-day horse drive to summer pasture in High Sierra Nevada. Seven-day professional packing school emphasizing wilderness livestock management also offered, as well as courses or educational trips in cooperation with area universities and organizations. Cost: $235-525 for scheduled trips, $390 for packing school.

**Stephen Biggs, Shasta Llamas, P.O. Box 1137, Mt. Shasta, CA 96067; (916) 926-3959.** Hiking trips in wilderness areas using llamas as pack animals, from June through September. Scheduled 3- and 5-day trips, custom 2- to 5-day trips, and spot-pack trips are offered, as well as combination raft/horsepack trips. Cost: $60/day for scheduled and custom trips, $30 one-way for spot-pack trips.

**Outing Dept., Sierra Club, 539 Bush St., San Francisco, CA 94108; (415)981-8634.** Eight-day summer hiking trips in the John Muir Wilderness using burros as pack animals. Participants themselves handle burros after lesson by guides on packing, unpacking, and handling them. Opportunity for fishing, photography, and exploring. Cost: $240.

**Ralph Heitman, Trinity Pack Trains, P.O. Box 277, Trinity Center, CA 96091; (916)266-3305. In winter: Rt. 1-89, McCoy Rd., Red Bluff, CA 96080; (916)527-5550.** Six- and 7-day horseback trips in the Trinity Alps Wilderness Area in summer. A leisurely pace is taken, with not more than 4 hours of riding per day, allowing time for fishing or side trips. Custom horseback, horsepack, spot-pack, or dunnage trips, or burro rental for hikers not needing guides are also available. Cost: $240-350 for scheduled trips, $50/guide/day and $18/pack-animal/day for spot-pack or dunnage trips.

**Dottie Moore or Mike McCoy, Wilderness Extension, University Extension, University of California, Davis, CA 95616; (916)752-3098.** Seven-day "living laboratory" horseback trip in the rugged alpine terrain of the Inyo and Sierra national forests to study wilderness horse husbandry; six-day field course on horseback in the High Sierra Nevada to study natural history of the area. No riding experience necessary; trips offered in summer. Cost: $445 for 7-day trip, includes 3 quarter credits; $425 for 6-day trip, includes 2 quarter credits.

# KAYAKING

From frozen glaciers in the High Cascades, Sawtooths, and Sierra Nevada, down the ever-widening river valleys that cut through Idaho desert, Oregon forest, and California meadow to the pulsing Pacific surf, water creates a channel of sustenance and sport. The kayak—with its shallow draw, light weight, and extreme maneuverability—is one of the best ways to explore the varied waterways of the Northwest. Pleasant to paddle in lakes and exciting in rapids, the kayak is making a bid to become the region's favorite recreational craft.

Developed in the arctic regions of North America, kayaks were originally long, narrow, skin-covered boats with decks covered to keep the ice hunter warm and the vessel seaworthy. Even the twin-bladed paddle used by today's kayakers was developed by the Eskimo, and capsized kayaks are righted by means of a technique known everywhere as the Eskimo roll. Today, the most common material for kayaks is fiberglass—easy to shape and repair and light enough to portage around difficult rapids or other obstructions. Though most kayakers are found on rivers, a good number like flat-water kayaking and racing, and a few go in for kayak surfing. There are even two-person kayaks for light recreational use and inflatable kayaks that are easy to pack in as additional gear on rafting trips.

Most kayaks are at least thirteen feet long, with seats and knee-and foot-braces built into the frame. Water skirts are often worn to prevent the added weight and discomfort of taking in water while going through rapids. Wet suits also may be worn, since white-water kayaking is an unavoidably chilly sport in cold spring run-off. Life jackets are required by federal regulations and helmets, especially those with good drainage and adequate protection of the temples, are recommended in white water.

As in most sports in which there's an element of danger, you should learn your skills well and never go out alone. White-water schools provide not only training in paddling, balance, and the Eskimo roll, but also the opportunity to meet others of your own level of experience and interest. There are also guided trips on the fjords of the British Columbia coastline, the wild and scenic Rogue River in Oregon, and the fast white water of the Skykomish River, an hour's drive from Seattle. On these and other trips in the Northwest, the experience gained in kayaking is supplemented by isolation, opportunity for wildlife observation, and the other pleasures of the wilderness, making kayaking among the most flexible and enjoyable of water sports.

# British Columbia

Brad Bradley, Brad's Tours, 401 E. Mercer #31, Seattle, WA 98102; (206)329-0227. Two-week kayaking trip on Portland Canal, 70-mile-long fjord separating British Columbia and Alaska, with 3,000-foot sheer rock walls at some points. Trip is offered in August and departs from and returns to Prince Rupert. A leisurely pace is taken, with layover time to hike, fish, clam, photograph, or relax. No experience necessary. Cost: $800. (TA)

Trekspeditions Adventure Travel, Ecosummer Canada, 207 W. Hastings St., suite 304, Vancouver, B.C., Canada V6B 1H7; (604)688-3921. Several ocean-kayaking trips in the Queen Charlotte Islands for 2 weeks and on the west coast of Vancouver Island for 10 or 11 days, in spring and summer. No previous experience necessary for most trips; trips are designed to be learning experiences. Excellent opportunity for observation of marine life, including marine mammals, and wildlife. Cost: $400-675. (TA)

Jim or Myrna Boulding, Strathcona Park Lodge and Outdoor Education Centre, Box 2160, Campbell River, B.C., Canada V9W 5C9; Campbell River radio, Strathcona Lodge 59 7021. Summer kayaking courses at all levels, ranging from weekend workshops to improve paddling techniques to 8-day west coast touring adventures, and from basic courses for beginners to instructors' clinics leading to certification for advanced paddlers. White-water programs emphasize safety and include instruction on how to read and navigate rapids and perform Eskimo rolls and kayak rescues. Cost: $100-400(Cdn.). (TA)

# Washington

Eric Sanford, Liberty Bell Alpine Tours,

Mazama, WA 98833; (509)996-2250. One-, 2-, and 5-day kayaking courses in summer for beginning and intermediate paddlers. Five-day program includes instruction in the Eskimo roll, basic strokes and turns, and both lake and river paddling. Cost: $40 for 1-day courses, $265 for 5-day courses. (TA)

James L. Moore or Michael Bellert, ORION Expeditions, Inc., 521 N. 72nd, Seattle, WA 98103; (206)782-8928. One-to 5-day kayak-touring expeditions in the San Juan Islands, on Ross Lake, on Lake Chelan, or along the Oregon coast from May through September. Close-knit, family atmosphere; trips are considered group activities, so participation is encouraged. Hearty meals are provided. Customized trips, such as combination bicycling/kayaking or hiking/kayaking, can be arranged. Cost: $42-375. (TA)

Jeff Utz, Outdoor Adventures, P.O. Box 500, Gold Bar, WA 98251; (206)282-8887. Five-day basic kayaking courses in summer, including instruction in reading the river, ferrying, and performing eddy turns and Eskimo rolls. Daily practice in quiet water alongside the instructor is followed by running different and increasingly difficult sections of several rivers during the week. By the end of the course each student should be able to handle white water of moderate difficulty. Cost: $685, includes food and lodging.

Doug Baker, White Water Sports, 307 N.E. 71st, Seattle, WA 98115; (206) 523-5150. Week-long kayaking camps in Wenatchee in summer. Daily trips on the White, Chiwawa, Wenatchee, and Skykomish rivers follow instruction in basic skills on Lake Wenatchee; evenings are spent in discussion of various aspects of the sport. Lodging and meals are provided in an inn on the shores of Lake Wenatchee or students can choose to camp. Round-trip transportation from Seattle is available. Also offered are classes in Seattle that meet on 4 weekday evenings and a weekend, and graduate overnight trips. Cost: $320 for Wenatchee camps, $125 for Seattle classes.

# Oregon

James H. Katz, James Henry River Journeys, P.O. Box 708, Stinson Beach, CA 94970; (415)525-6578 or 868-1836. Kayak school on the Rogue River in summer. Students may take 5-day beginning course, 5-day intermediate course, or 10-day combination course. Beginning course includes outings on the upper Rogue; entire intermediate course is actual experience on the river. Cost: $325 for 5-day courses, $600 for 10-day courses.

Gerald or Helen Bentley, Orange Torpedo Trips, P.O. Box 1111, Grants Pass, OR 97526; (503)479-5061. One- to 6-day guided inflatable-kayak trips on the Rogue and Deschutes rivers in Oregon, the Klamath River in California, and the Salmon River in Idaho, from June through mid-September. Each participant paddles his/her own kayak after instruction in boat-handling techniques and water safety procedures. Company pioneered commercial use of inflatable kayaks and is acknowledged authority on these craft. Cost: $200-250 for 3-day trips, $275 for 4-day trips, $390 for 6-day trips. (TA)

Michael R. Saul, Sundance Expeditions, Inc., 14894 Galice Rd., Merlin, OR 97532; (503)479-8508. Beginning kayaking courses on the Rogue River and intermediate courses on the Umpqua River in summer. Basic beginner's course is 9-day program terminating with 40-mile white-water trip on the lower Rogue. Five-day courses and private instruction are also available. Intermediate course lasts 3½ days, with 6 to 10 miles of river running each day. Accommodations and meals are provided at the Sundance Riverhouse, which borders the "Wild and Scenic" section of the Rogue River. Cost: $630 for 9-day basic courses, $300 for 5-day courses, $240 for 4-day intermediate courses. (TA)

Ted Birdseye, Sunrise Scenic Tours, 3791 Rogue River Hwy., Gold Hill, OR 97525; (503)582-0202. One- to 10-day kayaking courses in summer emphasizing rolling the kayak, reading the river, and gaining practical experience. Cost: $35 for 1 day, $130 for 2 days, $180 for 3 days, $250 for 4 days, $25 for each additional day. (TA)

**Joe or Sheila Leonard, Leonard Expeditions, Box 98, Stanley, ID 83278; (208) 774-3656.** Two-day and 5-day kayaking workshops on the Salmon River with student-to-instructor ratio never exceeding 5-to-2. Individualized instruction also available, as well as special clinics and events, including a 10-day expedition on the Owyhee River, a 4-day big-water clinic on the Salmon River, and a whitewater rodeo for paddlers from throughout the region. Cost: $150 for 2-day workshops, $300 for 5-day workshops, $600 for Owyhee River trip, $325 for big-water clinic.

**Gerald or Helen Bentley, Orange Torpedo Trips, P.O. Box 1111, Grants Pass, OR 97526; (503)479-5061.** See Oregon listing.

**University of California, Davis, CA 95616; (916)752-3098.** Beginning through intermediate kayaking courses in spring and summer. Weekend introductory or advanced beginning courses include practice on the American River, 5-day beginning and advanced beginning course includes long outings on the Klamath River, 5-day intermediate course offers instruction and practice in Class III and IV rapids on the Klamath River. Cost: $55-325.

**O.K. or Glenna Goodwin, World of Whitewater, P.O. Box 708, Big Bar, CA 96010; (916)623-6588 or 4110.** Kayaking instruction for beginners to advanced paddlers. One-day, weekend, and 5-day clinics offered from March through October. Custom-tailored group training programs, ranging from 1-day to week-long sessions, are available, as well as private lessons and guide service. Cost: $100 for weekend courses, $250 for 5-day courses.

# California

**Ann Dwyer, California Rivers, P.O. Box 468, Geyserville, CA 95441; (707)857-3872.** One-day kayak trip on the Russian River in May. Instruction is available. Cost: $50.

**James Katz, James Henry River Journeys, P.O. Box 708, Stinson Beach, CA 94970; (415)525-6578 or 868-1836.** See Oregon listing.

**Gerald or Helen Bentley, Orange Torpedo Trips, P.O. Box 1111, Grants Pass, OR 97526; (503)479-5061.** See Oregon listing.

**Ted Birdseye, Sunrise Scenic Tours, 3791 Rogue River Hwy., Gold Hill, OR 97525; (503)582-0202.** See Oregon listing.

**Dottie Moore or Mike McCoy, Wilderness Extension, University Extension,**

# MOUNTAINEERING

Most Americans consider the Rockies to be the continent's premier mountain range. Indeed, in Colorado alone there are fifty-four peaks over 14,000 feet high. Often, however, climbers from Colorado who come to the Northwest are amazed—and sometimes intimidated—by the mountaineering conditions here. Mount Elbert, Mount Massive, and Mount Harvard all may be higher than Mount Rainier, but it takes only a single look to know that the conditions that can be encountered while climbing the highest of the Cascade peaks are more demanding and variable, and ultimately more rewarding, than those found in the Rockies. For the rock climber, the ice climber, or the mountaineer who combines techniques on mixed terrain, the Northwest offers challenges that are impressive by any standard.

What motivates a person to climb is often questioned, especially by those for whom "exposure"—the absence of solid ground beneath one's feet for a considerable distance—seems an insurmountable obstacle. It might be just the satisfaction of reaching the summit, although that fails to explain the profound joy experienced by the technical rock climber in his skillful vertical dance up a sheer face. Through agility, strength, and balance, a competent climber can make an ascent up a seemingly featureless wall look as easy as walking down Broadway.

Climbing is a sport for all seasons, utilizing different tools and

techniques in summer than in winter. Gone are the pitons driven permanently into granite by the fair-weather climber of yesteryear; the pitons are replaced now by removable, reusable hexes and stoppers. Hammers and axes, ice screws and rigid crampons make it possible to climb straight up the crystalline face of a frozen waterfall in winter. As in the best of outdoor sports, aesthetics, as much as action itself, seems to enter into the activity.

But you don't have to be a Reinhold Messner or Jim Whittaker to climb in the Northwest. Schools that teach the basic holds and moves of technical climbing seem to have sprung up wherever there are rocks. Belaying your climbing partner during ascent and descending by extended rappels down steep walls are neither as difficult nor as frightening as they first seem, provided adequate teaching is available—and followed. Some programs can take you in a matter of days from the classroom to the glaciers or the summit, with full instruction in everything from mountain medicine and crevasse rescue to the knots, tools, and terminology of alpencraft.

With the variety of climbing conditions in the Northwest, a wide range of mountaineering options is available to the adventurous resident or visitor. Yosemite National Park has some of the most famous climbing routes in the country, such as those found on El Capitan. Mount Hood in Oregon offers a perfect training ground for all the mountaineering skills necessary to climb to the 11,235-foot summit. The classic Ptarmigan Traverse in the North Cascades of Washington crosses some of the nation's finest alpine terrain, most of it in the rugged and demanding world above timberline. In British Columbia, a series of high routes in the Bugaboos challenges both the rock and the ice climber. And in the Sawtooth National Recreation Area of Idaho, expeditions that last up to nine days provide the opportunity for extensive instruction in all the vital mountain skills.

The history of alpinism, from its eighteenth-century origins (in the Alps, of course) to its most dramatic successes in the Himalayas, is one of the most romantic in adventure sports. Sharing in that history is a benefit to anyone who climbs, whether it's on the flanks of Everest or in the Northwest's own mountains. Wherever there are mountains, there are mountaineers, participants in a sport that places value on a satisfying mixture of techniques and ethics, physical skill and spiritual awareness, set in an environment as wild and free as life itself.

# British Columbia

Loren Foss, Aerie Northwest, 4558 4th N.E., Seattle, WA 98105; (206)634-2849. A variety of mountaineering courses offered year-round with a multi-weekend format designed to prevent interference with work schedules and vacation plans. Courses include basic and winter mountaineering and ice and rock climbing. Special wilderness trips and custom guide service also available. Cost: $125-350 for courses, $195-240 for trips, $96-170 for guide service.

Roger Griffiths, Alpine Crafts Ltd., 1286 Kingsway, Vancouver, B.C., Canada V5V 3E1; (604)873-4915. Rock-climbing trips lasting 1 to 2 days in remote areas of British Columbia, such as Mt. Waddington, during spring and summer. Some experience required. Trips planned according to group's desires. Cost: $25/day. (TA)

John Carter, Arnica Adventure, R.R. 1, Nelson, B.C., Canada V1L 5P4; (604)825-9351. Six-day beginning and intermediate climbing trips operating out of a base camp in the West Kootenays in August and September. Good basic technique on mixed terrain, snow and ice work, and crevasse rescue are emphasized on beginners' trips; route finding, good mountain judgment, and developing confidence and skills in leading are emphasized on in-termediates' trips. Cost: $325(Cdn.) for beginners' trips, $395 for intermediates' trips. (TA)

Trekspeditions Adventure Travel, Ecosummer Canada, 207 W. Hastings St., suite 304, Vancouver, B.C., Canada V6B 1H7; (604)688-3921. Twelve-day trip in summer to Mt. Waddington, the apex of the Coast Range. Trip is designed to offer a balance between education and challenge, with a high priority placed on environmental awareness and knowledge of local ecology. Cost: available upon request. (TA)

Dunham Gooding, North Cascades Alpine School, 1212 24th St. W., Bellingham, WA 98225; (206)671-1505. A range of courses covering all aspects of alpine environment of interest to the mountaineer, including climbing fundamentals, expeditionary training, mountaineering medicine and rescue, and alpine ecology. Guided climbs are offered lasting from 2 to 7 days and ranging from basic climbs and traverses to demanding technical ascents. Cost: available upon request.

Arnör Larson, Northern Lights Alpine Recreation, Box 399, Invermere, B.C., Canada V0A 1K0; (604)342-6042. A variety of 8-day camps and ascents for all levels of mountaineering experience. Beginning camps from June to September provide basic mountaineering techniques, and backpack-in camps from July to September offer longer and more strenuous routes for intermediate and advanced

climbers. First ascents from May to October focus on a peak of over 3,000 meters. Two-week exploratory expeditions feature first ascent or a new route in trailless terrain. Participants provide their own food and equipment. Cost: $185-270(Cdn.) for camps, $300 for first ascents, $40/day for exploratory expeditions.

**Jim or Myrna Boulding, Strathcona Park Lodge and Outdoor Education Centre, Box 2160, Campbell River, B.C., Canada V9W 5C9; Campbell River radio, Strathcona Lodge 59 7021.** A number of rock- and ice-climbing courses and trips in Strathcona Park on Vancouver Island lasting 2 to 10 days. Programs range from short intensive classes in basic skills and an ice school on Comox and Cliffe glaciers to an ascent of the Golden Hinde, a strenuous trip for experienced backpackers. Trips offered out of Strathcona Lodge from May to October. Cost: $85-365(Cdn.). (TA)

# Washington

**Loren Foss, Aerie Northwest, 4558 4th N.E., Seattle, WA 98105; (206)634-2849.** See British Columbia listing.

**Jan Henderson or Stew Morton, Lute Jerstad Adventures, P.O. Box 19527, Portland, OR 97219; (503)244-4364.** Seminars in ice and rock climbing, alpine mountaineering, and mountain medicine and rescue offered from June through August. Student-to-instructor ratio is 4-to-1. Full-scale expeditions also scheduled each year. Cost: $275-375 for seminars. (TA)

**Ed Johann, Johann Mountain Guides, P.O. Box 2334, Lincoln City, OR 97367; (503)996-3232.** Many annual climbs, outings, and instructional programs led by seasoned mountaineer. Basic climbing schools include classroom instruction, field practice, and a summit climb of a major peak. Emphasis on personable and personalized service by family-run company. Trips offered year-round. Cost: $35/day. (TA)

**Eric Sanford, Liberty Bell Alpine Tours, Mazama, WA 98833; (509)996-2250.** Basic and advanced mountaineering, mountain leadership, and snow- and ice-climbing courses lasting 5 days offered in summer. Groups are kept very small with a low student-to-instructor ratio. College credit is available for mountain leadership course. Cost: $225-260.

**Darryl Lloyd, Mt. Adams Wilderness Institute, Flying L Ranch, Glenwood, WA 98619; (509)364-3511.** Eight- and 12-day wilderness mountaineering courses on Mt. Adams. Students are instructed in mountaineering techniques, wilderness travel, and alpine environment and are totally involved in all phases of the mountaineering expedition. Trips are offered from June through August and begin at family-operated guest ranch southeast of Portland. Cost: $400 for 8-day courses, $500 for 12-day courses.

**Dunham Gooding, North Cascades Alpine School, 1212 24th St. W., Bellingham, WA 98825; (206)671-1505.** See British Columbia listing.

**Jeff Utz, Outdoor Adventures, Box 500, Gold Bar, WA 98251; (206)282-8887 or 793-1166.** Three-day rock-climbing seminars in the Leavenworth area of the Cascades to cover fundamental techniques, and 5-day seminars in the Mt. Stuart Range to learn rock and ice techniques in changeable conditions. Instructor is world-class climber. Trips offered from July to September. Cost: $168 for 3-day seminars, $278 for 5-day seminars.

**W. Gerald Lynch, Rainier Mountaineering, Inc., 201 St. Helens Ave., Tacoma, WA 98402; (206)627-6242.** Three-day summit climbs of Mt. Rainier consist of 1-day snow- and ice-climbing school and 2-day climb. Five-day snow- and ice-climbing seminars, 1-day crevasse rescue courses, and 6-day expedition seminars offered from May to September. Five-day winter-mountaineering classes also available. Cost: $125 for Rainier climbs, $30 for 1-day seminars, $225 for 5-day seminars, $300 for 6-day seminars. (TA)

# Oregon

Richard Arend, Exploregon, 9603 S.W. Taylor, Portland, OR 97225; (503)292-8991. Several different trips to the central Oregon Cascades, combining climbing instruction with enjoyment of the wilderness. Climbs include 6 days on the South Sister and 3 days on Mt. Hood. Three-day trips to the Columbia Gorge include rock climbing, hiking, and boating; accommodations provided at an inn. Trips offered from May to October. Cost: $215 for 3-day trips, $410 for 6-day trips, and $315 for Columbia Gorge trips. (TA)

Jan Henderson or Stew Morton, Lute Jerstad Adventures, P.O. Box 19527, Portland, OR 97219; (503)244-4364. See Washington listing.

Ed Johann, Johann Mountain Guides, P.O. Box 2334, Lincoln City, OR 97367; (503)996-3232. See Washington listing.

# Idaho

Lyman C. Dye, EE-DA-HOW Mountaineering and Guide Service, P.O. Box 207, Ucon, ID 83454; (208)523-9276. Guided ascents and 1-day training sessions in the Sawtooth National Recreation Area. One-day climbs cover basic, intermediate, or advanced techniques; longer climbs include 4-, 6-, and 9-day expeditions with more extensive instruction. Climbs offered from June to September. Winter climbs by special arrangement. Cost:

$15-30 for 1-day courses, $145-320 for longer trips.

# California

Terry Halbert, Mountain People School, 157 Oak Spring Dr., San Anselmo, CA 94960; (415)457-3664. Basic introduction to rock climbing through instruction and progressively more difficult climbs over 2 days. Class is held on weekends. Cost: $35, includes transportation from San Rafael and all equipment.

Palisade School of Mountaineering, P.O. Box 694, Bishop, CA 93514; (714)935-4330. Broad spectrum of mountain courses and guided climbs in the most alpine region of the Sierra Nevada. Five-day basic and advanced rock-climbing courses and 7-day basic and advanced mountaineering courses are offered in summer. Maximum of 3 students per instructor. Other offerings include mountain medicine and avalanche awareness seminars. Cost: $555 for basic courses, $205 for avalanche seminars, $215 for mountain medicine seminars.

Yosemite Mountaineering School and Guide Service, Yosemite National Park, CA 95389; (209)372-4611 ext. 244. Guided climbs and special seminars on various aspects of mountaineering offered from March to September. Basic courses last 1 to 4 days; seminars include a week-long alpencraft session, providing a complete mountaineering background with instruction in rock, ice, and snow climbing and survival techniques. Cost: $16-30 for short courses, $150 for alpencraft seminar, $35/day for guided climbs, includes instruction or guide only.

# NATURE
# WATCHING

Just about every adventure trip in the Northwest can be a nature-watching one. Whether you're soaring on thermals in a sailplane, diving to sunken cargo, or backpacking along the Pacific Crest Trail, the world of nature surrounds you. Many people take part in adventure trips just for this reason. Rediscovering the natural world puts you in touch with a part of your own nature that is too often buried in modern life.

Many trips in the Northwest are designed to explore the expressions of nature. Birds are the subject of many nature-watching trips. The Pacific Flyway, a waterfowl migration route between Alaskan nesting grounds and winter roosts in California and Mexico, lies over the Northwest. Several sanctuaries and refuges have been established to maintain stable gathering points for these migrating birds, which include trumpeter and whistling swans, sandhill cranes, snow and Canada geese, and various species of ducks. Preserves at Malheur National Wildlife Refuge in southeastern Oregon and Creston Valley Wildlife Management Area in British Columbia are but two sites where educational programs and field studies are available.

More rugged nature-watching trips also are possible. At Strathcona Provincial Park on Vancouver Island, you can canoe or backpack along the island's west coast to explore the intertidal life zone by digging for clams and oysters, fishing for salmon and cod, watching for gray and killer whales off the coast, and discussing Stone Age whale-hunting tech-

niques that the Nootka Indians originated on these beaches. Or you can take a seagoing trip in which you ply the very waters the whales do for a close-up and informative look at the marine mammals of the Northwest.

Nature-watching trips differ from other adventures in that they are less concerned with the excitement of the outdoors than with its significance. Consequently, participants tend to be of much different ages and have a wider range of experiences to contribute to the trip. Guides invariably are specialists in their fields—many have done postdoctoral work, and a few are authors or photographers of some note. When you sign up for a nature-watching trip, you are virtually ensured of having an informative and stimulating learning experience that goes beyond the textbooks of the classroom into the open book of the natural world.

# British Columbia

**Creston Valley Wildlife Management Area, Box 640, Creston, B.C., Canada V0B 1G0; (604)428-9319.** Wildlife management area was created to preserve and improve waterfowl habitat for the birds of the Pacific Flyway. Wildlife Centre has a variety of displays and offers naturalist-led exploration, on foot or by canoe, slide shows, nature walks, and demonstrations. Programs can be tailored to suit the needs of groups. The area is open year-round, but January and February have least waterfowl activity. Bird species in the valley number approximately 240. Cost: available upon request.

**Trekspeditions Adventure Travel, Eco-summer Canada, 207 W. Hastings St., suite 304, Vancouver, B.C., Canada V6B 1H7; (604)688-3921.** Many diverse nature-watching trips offered, including kayaking trips to observe and photograph birds in their nesting habitat in the Queen Charlotte Islands; backpacking trips to observe and photograph mountain wildlife, with study of resident flora and geological history; touring-kayak trips to Kingcome Inlet to observe and photograph bald eagles and eulachon, or candlefish. Trips are offered from April through September; custom-tailored trips can be arranged. Cost: $230-635. (TA)

# Washington

**Brad Bradley, Brad's Tours, 401 E. Mercer #31, Seattle, WA 98102; (206)329-0227.** Seven-day "Washington Wildflower Safari" in the Cascade and Olympic mountains in July with a professional naturalist escort. A variety of plant habitats is visited, so a great variety and profusion of blooms are seen. Three nights lodging in Seattle and an Indian salmon bake are included. Cost: $600. (TA)

**John Bierlein, Discovery Park, 3801 W. Government Way, Seattle, WA 98199; (206)625-4636.** Nature walks in Discovery Park at 2:00 P.M. each Saturday year-round and on weekdays by special arrangement. Topics of discussion include such things as mushrooms, wild edibles, forest ecology, and birds. Cost: free.

**Jim Styers, Specialty Tours, 19724 N.E. 181st, Woodinville, WA 98072; (206) 788-3267.** Three-day trips for marine-mammal watching from 65-foot boat offered from June through September. Several guides are experts on marine mammals; many species of marine mammals are observed. A visit to a whale museum and evening slide shows and discussions are included. Cost: $155.

# Oregon

**Malheur Environmental Field Station, P.O. Box 989, Burns, OR 97720.** Malheur National Wildlife Refuge was set aside as a nesting area for migratory birds and also is a gathering point for waterfowl of the Pacific Flyway in spring and fall. Outstanding assembly of birds and other wildlife makes the refuge, which is open to visitors year-round, an excellent area for wildlife study. The Environmental Field Station is operated by Oregon colleges and universities and offers field-oriented courses in such subjects as geology, ecology, mammalogy, and botany during the summer. Cost: available upon request.

# Idaho

**Boyd  E.  Norton  or  Lynn  Benson,**

**Wilderness Photography Workshops, University of the Wilderness, P.O. Box 1687, Evergreen, CO 80439; (303)674-9724.** Seven-day nature photography workshops at remote Shepp Ranch on the banks of the Salmon River in April and May; 7-day combination photography workshop/river-raft trip on the Salmon River in May. Abundant wildflowers and wildlife, including bighorn sheep, deer, elk, bear, eagles. Photographers of all levels of accomplishment are welcome; director is highly acclaimed wilderness photographer. Cost: $750 for Shepp Ranch workshop, $950 for combination trip.

# California

**Outing Dept., Sierra Club, 530 Bush St., San Francisco, CA 94108; (415)981-8634.** Various educational outings with a well-defined program led by a naturalist. Cost: $200.

# PARACHUTING

Why would anyone want to jump out of a plane? The fear of falling is one of the mind's insurmountable barriers. Yet each year thousands of people voluntarily leap from an airplane soaring 5,000 feet over the earth, with nothing between them and the ground but thin air and a parachute. It may be that you have to try parachuting to understand it, because those who do it return to earth with glowing reports of the sense of freedom earned in their first jump—and many of them are eager to jump again.

Safety is, of course, a prime concern and is the focus of all Northwest parachute training schools. The equipment is usually of the highest quality and the parachutes are packed by experts to ensure that they will work properly. The chutes are made of high quality nylon and are rigged to a comfortable harness system that permits easy in-the-air maneuvering. Trainees are taught how to jump from an aircraft, how to check to see if the chute is properly deployed, how to maneuver by following ground instructions, and how to land in the least bone-jarring way. A ground crew monitors the progress of the first-time chutist and, by moving a large arrow visible from the skies, relays instructions to make sure the landing is far away from obstacles. Most of the landings are no worse than a ten-foot drop.

Lectures by experienced parachutists, audio-visual aids such as slide shows and movies, and on-site training in falling and landing—as well as that initial plunge itself—are included in the cost of a first-jump course. Often those who have made it describe the biggest surprise as the haunting sense that the fall may go on forever, and they may never reach the earth below. Then there is a sharp jerk as the chute is automatically deployed, the frantic rushing of wind seems to halt, and the sense of falling is transformed into a sense of controlled flight.

Then there's time to look around—at the rolling hills, the snow-capped peaks in the distance, the signposts of civilization spread out below like a map come to life. When at last the landing is made, you may look for the nearest airplane, ready to climb aboard for another try. And the fear of falling may be transformed into an almost addictive urge to make more jumps from the heavens to the earth, to explore the thrills of free fall and the pleasures of relative work with other sky-divers in the dreamlike adventure of parachuting.

# British Columbia

**David Payne, Invermere Sky Divers, Box 51, Athalmer, B.C., Canada V0A 1A0; (604)342-6521 or 9246.** Parachuting instruction by arrangement. Cost: $100 for training, $15/jump for experienced parachutists.

# Washington

**Ken Eskeback or Marilyn Imhof, Toledo Parachute Center, P.O. Box 7, Toledo, WA 98591; (206)864-2555.** First-jump and novice training and facilities for experienced parachutists near Mt. St. Helens. Open year-round. Cost: $75 for training.

# Oregon

**Pacific Parachute Center, P.O. Box 237, Sheridan, OR 97378; (503)843-3616.** Parachute center is one of the largest in the U.S. and is open daily year-round. Basic 15-jump course goes through static-line jumps up through free falls. Cost: $70 for 1st jump, $15 for static-line jumps (minimum of 5), $13 for free falls; $4-10/jump for experienced parachutists.

# Idaho

**Ozmo Paracenter, Inc., Rt. 1, Box 63,**

Athol, ID 83801; (208)683-2821. U.S.P.A.-affiliated parachute center offers 1st-jump through advanced lessons on weekends in summer. Cost: $80 for 1st jump, $20/jump for subsequent jumps.

# California

Dave or Carol Rudolph, Corning Drop Zone, Rt. 1 Box 714, Durham, CA 95938; (916)891-1084. Personalized first-jump and novice training offered; facilities available for experienced parachutists. Open year-round, weather permitting. Cost: $48-65 for training.

Pope Valley Parachute Center, 1996 Pope Canyon Rd., Pope Valley, CA 94567; (707)965-3400. All phases of parachute jumping, including training, offered year-round. Cost: $75 for training; $8-11/jump for experienced parachutists; $15 for equipment rental.

# RESEARCH/STUDY EXPEDITIONS

Science has always depended heavily on research. Inspiration, theory, and proof all derive to one degree or another from the challenging process of gathering information, collating details, accumulating data. With the material gathered in the field—whether it be the small pea patch in Mendel's backyard or the vast heavens opened up to Galileo through the telescope—people of genius make strides in human knowledge.

A fairly recent innovation in scientific research has been the use of volunteers, with little or no formal training, as field workers in research projects. While on the job, they learn the necessary data-gathering techniques, from sifting through sand for tiny traces of human habitation at archaeological dig sites to following the daily routine of endangered species in their natural surroundings. Their contribution to the advancement of science already has proved to be of enormous value and will no doubt continue to do so in the years to come.

For the volunteer, such projects offer a rare opportunity to get in on the ground floor of scientific endeavor and a chance to spend days or weeks in a stimulating and often beautiful field environment. Working with wildlife specialists on Vancouver Island, for example, team interns examine firsthand the habitat needs and behavior of three wild-land species: wolves, deer, and elk. A small backpacking study group examines the remote clear-water wild lands adjoining the Idaho Primitive Area, trying to answer perplexing questions about the endangered species in this fragile ecological region.

Besides the expeditions that contribute to ongoing scientific research programs, there also are many trips of a more academic nature. Some even are available for college credit in fields from biology to writing, environmental studies to art. Carrying all the necessary study materials, including textbooks, field guides, and cameras, you go deep into the back-country. Under the tutelage of scientists, you can learn about alpine ecology in the mountains of California, glaciology in the North Cascades, or vegetation and wildlife along the Snake River on the Oregon-Idaho border. Studying photography in the school of Ansel Adams in Yosemite Valley or nature writing such as that of Joseph Wood Krutch or Edward Abbey while in the High Sierra Nevada provides a satisfying combination of personal expression and education in an inspirational environment. Whether you mine the wild lands for data on endangered species, or your own spirit for personal revelation, research or study expeditions can be a key to appreciating the Northwest.

# British Columbia

Anne Keiter, Expedition Training Institute, Inc., Box 171 NAG, Prudential Center, Boston, MA 02199; (617)922-0577. Research expeditions in the natural and environmental sciences for 16- to 26-year-olds. Expeditions are scheduled in January and summer for 2 weeks to 1 month. Scholarships and graduate or undergraduate college credit are available. Cost: $900/month.

Jeanne Ragan, Wildlands Research Institute, University of California Extension, Santa Cruz, CA 95064; (408) 429-2822. Students join small backcountry research teams as working field interns on wildlife, wild-land, and wild-river projects during the summer. Previous experience not required; necessary skills taught on site. Students earn 5 quarter credits. Cost: $500, includes tuition only; food and on-site transportation costs are shared.

# Washington

David Birkner, American Field Studies, 2301 W. Raye St., Seattle, WA 98199; (206)282-2301. A variety of field courses on such topics as natural history, ecology, or historical geography of specific areas, or such special topics as children and the world of nature, or songs of birds. Courses offer academic credit and are held in spring, summer, and fall. Cost: $75-150. (TA)

Anne Keiter, Expedition Training Institute, Inc., Box 171 NAG, Prudential Center, Boston, MA 02199; (617)922-0577. See British Columbia listing.

# Oregon

David Birkner, American Field Studies, 2301 W. Raye St., Seattle, WA 98199; (206)282-2301. See Washington listing.

Malheur Environmental Field Station, P.O. Box 989, Burns, OR 97720. Malheur National Wildlife Refuge was set aside as a nesting area for migratory birds and also is a gathering point for waterfowl of the Pacific Flyway in spring and fall. Outstanding assembly of birds and other wildlife makes the refuge, which is open to visitors year-round, an excellent area for wildlife study. The Environmental Field Station is operated by Oregon colleges and universities and offers field-oriented courses in such subjects as geology, ecology, mammalogy, and botany during the summer. Cost: available upon request.

Jeanne Ragan, Wildlands Research Institute, University of California Extension, Santa Cruz, CA 95064; (408)429-2822. See British Columbia listing.

# Idaho

Jeanne Ragan, Wildlands Research Institute, University of California Extension, Santa Cruz, CA 95064; (408)429-2822. See British Columbia listing.

# California

Anne Keiter, Expedition Training Institute, Inc., Box 171 NAG, Prudential Center, Boston, MA 02199; (617)922-0577. See British Columbia listing.

Jeanne Ragan or Susan Powell, Sierra Institute, University Extension, University of California, Santa Cruz, CA 95064; (408)429-2822. Interdisciplinary wilderness studies in the Sierra backcountry for undergraduate liberal arts students. Spring, summer, and fall courses in natural history, ecology, nature photography, wilderness history, aesthetics, and philosophy, with the goal of direct comprehensive knowledge of wilderness and the wilderness experience. Summer courses offer 5 quarter credits; spring and fall courses offer 15 credits. Cost: $180 for summer courses, $350 for spring and fall courses, includes tuition only; food and on-site transportation costs shared.

Dottie Moore or Mike McCoy, Wilderness Extension, University Extension, University of California, Davis, CA 95616; (916)752-3098. Avian and natural history field courses led by naturalists offered in spring and summer. Topics include such things as northern California raptors, wintering birds of Honey Lake, and natural history of the Tioga Pass/Mono Lake region. Courses offered for academic credit. Cost: $50-425.

Jeanne Ragan, Wildlands Research Institute, University of California Extension, Santa Cruz, CA 95064; (408)429-2822. See British Columbia listing.

Henry Berrey, Yosemite Natural History Association, P.O. Box 545, Yosemite National Park, CA 95389; (209)372-4532. A variety of field seminars designed to provide knowledge of plant and animal life and the spectacular geology of Yosemite National Park. Most courses are accredited through the University Extension, University of California, Davis; academic credit is available. Instructors are natural history teachers at California colleges, experienced ranger-naturalists, or outstanding instructors in their fields. Cost: $35-80.

# RIVER CRUISING

River rafting is for those who crave the excitement of active participation in white water. River cruising, on the other hand, is for those who want a more relaxed, informative experience. Where the white water is enormous or the river canyons long and remote, a jet boat is the most practical way to experience a river. In placid water, on the other hand, where the scenery is special and the river's heritage valuable, a more gentle motor cruise may be called for.

Perhaps the region's most famous river is the Columbia. Lewis and Clark explored it as a route to the Pacific 175 years ago; Woody Guthrie celebrated it in song. It is a source of vast electrical energy, an artery of commerce, and a valuable scenic attraction. A large, well-equipped sightseeing vessel cruises the Columbia for a leisurely look at its historical sites, Indian heritage, energy powerhouses, and the incomparable beauty of the Columbia Gorge, on the border between Washington and Oregon.

If you still want to experience some of the excitement of white water, then a jet boat may be the vehicle for you. Jet boats are fast, comfortable craft that can run upstream as well as down and, since they have no propellers, can skim rapidly through shallow water. On Idaho's Salmon River, the "River of No Return," plenty of wildlife and towering mountains vie for attention with old abandoned miners' cabins and Indian sites. The nearby Snake River cuts through Hells Canyon, the deepest river gorge in North America; the geological record exposed over the ninety-mile stretch of river can be toured by jet boat in just a few short hours.

The Rogue River in southern Oregon is the setting for another popular cruise. It offers white water for the action enthusiast, extended placid stretches ideal for salmon or steelhead fishing, and such wildlife as ospreys, bald eagles, black-tailed deer, and otters. The Klamath River of northern California is the avenue for a sixty-four-mile jet-boat tour into redwood country, with an option available for an overnight stopover at a secluded lodge.

Most cruise boat operators provide lunch and rest stops for swimming, photography, and socializing. Hikes may be made to nearby Indian petroglyphs, abandoned mines, or exposed ancient lava flows. Informed guides, rapid transportation, and often spectacular scenery are the constants that contribute to the popularity of Northwest river cruises.

# Washington

# Oregon

Ann or Ernie Duckworth, Ernie's Hells Canyon Tours, 3010 Riverside Dr., Clarkston, WA 99403; (509)758-9831. One-day, 184-mile jet-boat cruises offered from May through October. Trips are planned around interests of guests; opportunity for swimming, exploring, gold panning. Meals are provided. Optional additonal 12-mile white-water trip offered from July through September for an extra charge. Cost: $90.

Floyd or Grayce Held, Held's Canyon Tours, 118 Sycamore St., Clarkston, WA 99403; (509)758-3445. One-day, 180-mile, white-water cruises offered from April through November. Trips include visits to abandoned mines, Indian campgrounds, and historical sites, and opportunities to see exposed lava flows, Indian petroglyphs, and wildlife. Meals are provided. Cost: $75.

Garry Cassidy, Columbia Sightseer, P.O. Box 307, Cascade Locks, OR 97014; (503) 374-8474 or 8619. Daily 2½-hour tours on the Columbia River in summer; 4½-hour to 7-day cruises on the Columbia, Snake, and Willamette rivers in fall and spring. All trips include narration on history, river commerce, geology, Indian life and legends, etc. Two-day "Short Course on the Columbia," accredited by Washington State University Extension Service, also offered. Group or private charters available year-round. Cost: $6 for 2½-hour cruises; $30 for 4½-hour cruises; $145 for 2-day cruises; $120-150 for short course. (TA)

Court Boice, Court's White Water Trips, P.O. Box 1045, Gold Beach, OR 97444; (503)247-6504. Jet-boat cruises on the Rogue River offered from April 1 to November 1. Round trip of 64 miles can be made in 4 or 6 hours, and white-water round trip of 104 miles can be made in 8 hours or 2 days, according to guests' choice. Two-day trip includes overnight stay at wilderness lodge. Cost: $15 for 64-mile cruises; $35 for 8-hour, 104-mile cruises; $42 for 2-day, 104-mile cruises. (TA)

**Gary Woolsey, Hellgate Excursions, Inc., P.O. Box 982, Grants Pass, OR 97526; (503)479-7204.** Two-hour scenic cruises, 4-hour "Country Dinner Excursions," and 5-hour "Rough Water Trips" through Hellgate Canyon on the Rogue River offered from May 15 through September 30. Four-hour trips feature outdoor barbecue dinner. Cost: $10 for 2-hour trips; $23 for 4-hour trips, includes dinner; $25 for 5-hour trips.

**Ed Kammer, Mail Boat Wild Water Trips, P.O. Box 1181, Gold Beach, OR 97444; (503)247-6225 or 7972.** Daily 104-mile trips on the Rogue River, including wild white-water section, offered from May 15 to October 15, in jet boats that carry mail to isolated inhabitants of the upper Rogue. Guides provide narration on wildlife, botany, gold mining, and Indian lore. Lunch stop provides time for hiking, swimming, or fishing. Cost: $40.

# Idaho

**Stephen Dixon, Salmon River Lodge, Inc., P.O. Box 348, Jerome, ID 83338; (208)324-3553 or 5568.** Daily jet-boat trips on the Salmon River for parties of 6 to 20 persons, available by reservation. Opportunity for fishing, gold panning, photography, wildlife observation. Cost: determined by number in party and length of trip. (TA)

# California

**Alvin or Juanita Larson, Klamath Jet Boats, Inc., P.O. Box 5, Klamath, CA 95548; (707)482-4191 or 4422.** Daily 6-hour jet-boat trips on primitive section of Klamath River. Opportunity for wildlife observation. Guests can have camping gear transported or stay overnight at lodge if they wish. Custom trips available for large groups. Cost: $20.

# RIVER RAFTING

Few adventure trips are as popular as river rafting. The reasons are many—rivers are found worldwide, cutting through landscapes as diverse as the earth has to offer, and support an abundance of wildlife. All of these benefits can be enjoyed while rafting in the company of friends aboard a practically unsinkable craft, in comically sloppy or elegantly precise river runs. You don't have to be an expert, an athlete, or a child to have the time of your life.

The rafts professionals use for commercial trips range in length from twelve to twenty-one feet and are made of rubberized neoprene or more durable synthetics such as Hypalon. They can be inflated to near rigidity, an essential quality for safe rough-water use.

There are two basic crewing options in river rafting, and most trip operators will use both on the same outing if it is safe. Paddle rafts are crewed by the customers themselves, most of whom have never been on any sort of river trip. A guide instructs the crew in the basic commands and paddle strokes, then steers the craft downstream through rapids of up to Class IV or even V difficulty (on a scale of I to VI, Class VI is virtually unrunnable). Most people in reasonably good physical condition find this an exciting way to participate in the adventure of rafting, because it gives them a real feel of the force and subtleties of white water.

The second option is the oarboat, which is rowed downstream by the guide and loaded with supplies as well as those customers who would rather concentrate on the unfolding scenery than paddle commands. Most nature-oriented trips, such as excursions to see bald eagles on the Skagit or the geologically fascinating float down the John Day, are oared floats, as are the other extreme, wild white-water runs down the Class V Salmon or Snake in Idaho. Generally, at least one oarboat comes on each river trip—more if the venture is an overnighter or longer—to carry food, safety equipment, and spare clothing and gear.

Life jackets, usually supplied by the trip operator, are required equipment on all river journeys because the possibility that a passenger may fall out is never entirely absent. Hats or caps are recommended for protection against the sun or rain, and safety straps for your glasses are a good idea. Because hypothermia is always a potential problem on river trips in winter or early spring, wet suits also are advisable. But during the rest of the year, if the weather is good, cut-offs, T-shirts, and tennis shoes are sufficient clothing. Most guides are trained in first aid and water safety and are well versed in river lore as well—the geologic history, trees, wildlife, plants, and the stories behind old miners' shacks, homesteads, and logging camps.

Since there are so many different trip options, and since rafting is the single most popular adventure activity in the Northwest, we have described the rivers by state and province. This will give you more information on which to base your decision of which trip or trips to take. Naturally some rivers, such as the Grande Ronde in Oregon and Washington and the Snake between Idaho and Oregon, flow across or along state borders. In these cases, the river is listed in the state of its origin—Oregon for the Grande Ronde, Idaho for the Snake. But look through all of the descriptions—there are many more rivers to raft, and many more facets of the Northwest to explore, than you may have imagined.

# British Columbia

British Columbia is a land of superlatives. Its coastline is among the most wild and rugged on the continent. Its mountains are among the highest and most densely forested. Its rivers are no less impressive. The Fraser is one of the longest and deepest in North America, with average flows of 150,000 cubic feet per second (compared with 8,000 to 15,000 for many of the Northwest's other rivers). Some of the most abundant salmon runs in the world are found on its tributaries.

The Chilko, a high tributary of the Fraser, drops 100 feet per mile for fifteen miles. Beginning upstream, it offers Class V-plus white water—and Class VI is usually considered unrunnable. The river has been preserved from damming by the quality of its sockeye run—fully a third of the sockeye that return to the Fraser spawn at the drainage of Chilko Lake. Some of the river's sixty-five miles can be canoed, but the fifteen miles of Lava Canyon can be run only by experts in inflatable rafts. The river then continues northward and loses itself in the Chilcotin —although the Chilcotin's flow at the confluence is substantially less than that of its tributary, the Chilko.

The Chilcotin is a less aggressive river, its waters warmer and drops lower than those of the Chilko. It cuts across the Fraser Plateau, an area of lava flows and dense riverside growth, and its Class III and IV rapids vie for attention with mountain sheep and sculpted sandhills called "hoodoos." The eleven miles from Farwell to the Fraser are the river's fastest and include the Class IV Farwell Rapids and the Class V Railroad Rapids, formed in 1973 by a huge slide off the canyon wall. Most Chilcotin trips continue onto the Fraser and use large, motorized inflatables to cope with the powerful hydraulics of the grandfather of Canadian rivers. Its rapids—Bridge River, Hell's Gate, and others—are substantial, and the landscape varies from sage and cactus desert to forested canyons farther downriver. Chil-cotin-Fraser trips generally last about a week.

Another tributary of the Fraser, the Thompson, provides a shorter (one to three days) white-water experience amidst rolling hills of sagebrush, jack pine, and cactus, and waterfalls that grace the white sandstone canyon walls. Sand beaches are used for lunch stops and campsites. In southeastern British Columbia, the Kootenay River, flowing out of the Canadian Rockies, is the site for a one- or two-day trip through Class II and III white water and unsurpassed scenery. Although damming has limited the wildness of the river, much of its character and wildlife remain to be enjoyed on a scenic, if brief, adventure.

**Stephen L. Cutright, American River Touring Assoc., 1307 Harrison St., Oakland, CA 94612; (415)465-9355.** Six- and 10-day trips on the Chilko, Chilcotin, and Fraser rivers, June through September, using motorized rafts. Cost: $400 for 6-day trips, $975 for 10-day trips.

**Brian McDonald, Black Tusk Touring and Guide Service Ltd., 3064 St. Kildas Ave., N. Vancouver, B.C., Canada V7N 2A9; (604)985-9223.** One- and 2-day trips on the Fraser or Thompson rivers and 6-day trips on the Chilcotin and Fraser offered May through October. Cost: $50 for 1-day trips, $145 for 2-day trips, $375 for 6-day trips.

**John H. Mikes, Canadian River Expeditions Ltd., 845 Chilco St., suite 401, Vancouver, B.C., Canada V6G 2R2; (604)926-4436.** Ten-day trips encompassing a cruise of parts of the Inside Passage, a plane ride over the Coast Range, and 200 miles of white-water rafting on the Chilko, Chilcotin, and Fraser rivers offered July through September. Cost: $975(U.S.). (TA)

**Daryl or Linda Bespflug, Kootenay River Runners, P.O. Box 81, Edgewater, B.C., Canada V0A 1E0; (604)347-9210.** One- and 2-day wilderness raft trips on the

Kootenay River in summer featuring small groups and personalized service. Cost: $50 for 1-day trips, $145 for 2-day trips. (TA)

**Bernie Fandrich, Kumsheen Raft Adventures Ltd., Box 339, Main St., Lytton, B.C., Canada V0K 1Z0; (604)455-2410.** One- to 8-day trips on the Fraser, Thompson, and Chilcotin rivers, May through September. One option is 5-day guest-ranch/rafting holiday; some trips offered in conjunction with University of British Columbia Continuing Education Center.

Cost: $65/day. (TA)

**Sandra duBrule, Safari Expeditions, Ltd., 969 W. Broadway, Vancouver, B.C., Canada V5Z 1K3; (604)738-5917.** One- and 2-day expeditions on the Thompson River and 5-day trips on the Fraser, April through October. Cost: $59(Cdn.) for 1-day trips, $129 for 2-day trips, $520 for 5-day trips. (TA)

**Ron Thompson, Thompson Guiding Ltd., Riske Creek, B.C., Canada V0L 1T0; (604)659-5635.** Seven-day wilderness-oriented trips encompassing both the Chilko and Chilcotin rivers, mid-June through mid-September. Trips include the Chilko's 1500-foot drop in 15 miles. Cost: $635. (TA)

**Dan Culver, Whitewater Adventures Ltd., 105 W. 6th Ave., Vancouver, B.C., Canada V5Y 1K3; (604)879-6701.** One- and 2-day trips on the Thompson or Fraser rivers, April through October, and 6-day trips on the Chilcotin and Fraser in July and August. Cost: $50 for 1-day trips, $120 for 2-day trips, $425 for 6-day trips. (TA)

**Richard or Rochelle Wright, Wright's River Explorations, 549 Ioco Rd., Port Moody, B.C., Canada V3H 2W3; (604) 461-6361.** One-, 2-, and 3-day trips on the Thompson River from late May to September; 3- and 5-day trips on the Fraser in August; and 2- and 6-day trips on the Chilcotin in June and July. Cost: $60 for 1-day trips, $130 for 2-day trips, $175-240 for 3-day trips, $390-420 for 5-day trips, $490 for 6-day trips.

# Washington

Most Washington rivers are too short to allow overnight trips, so one-day floats are the rule. This is due to the rivers' relatively steep drop out of the Cascade and Olympic mountains to inhabited flatlands. But the white water is among the most enjoyable in the Northwest, flowing through dense conifer forests, with views of impressive mountain ridges and peaks not uncommon.

The rivers of the Cascade Range generally flow east to west, toward Puget Sound and the Pacific. The best white water is found on the Skykomish, a mere hour's drive from Seattle. Put-in is at the base of a climber's dream, towering Mount Index, and the run itself includes several Class IV rapids and one Class V—Boulder Drop, the toughest in the state. Consistently strong currents and multiple obstacles make the "Sky" a thrilling, and sometimes risky, run. Farther north, the "wild and scenic" rivers of the Skagit system—the Suiattle, the Sauk, and the Skagit itself—inspire a real wilderness feeling due to the mature, sparsely inhabited forests through which they flow. The Suiattle is a small but dynamic Class III river with no bridges, houses, or visible roads along its fourteen-mile length. The upper Sauk is an infrequently run Class IV river, known locally as the "little Sky," while the lower Sauk and the Skagit are ideal for natural history floats in winter. Then, up to four hundred bald eagles visit the area to feed on spawned-out salmon. The Skagit, incidentally, offers some of the best salmon and steelhead fishing in the state.

On the eastern flank of the Cascades, the Methow River's twenty-mile route through the Black Canyon and the Wenatchee River's fourteen-mile run are favorites. The roller-coaster ride on the Wenatchee features rapids bordering on Class IV at high water, including Rock 'n Roll and Snowblind, while waves over eight feet high make Drunkard's Drop and Gorilla perennial favorites.

On the Olympic Peninsula, much quieter floats are available on the Queets, Hoh, and Quinault rivers, which run through the Olympic National Park's rain forest. The forest receives up to two hundred inches of rain per year—most of it during rafting's off-season, be assured—and the Douglas fir, red cedar, western hemlock, and Sitka spruce vegetation rivals tropical rain forests in the denseness of its canopy. Wildlife from otter to elk is often spotted during early morning or late afternoon or on overcast days. Ospreys and an occasional bald eagle may be glimpsed in the treetops. The Hoh River float is unique in that its take-out is on the beach at the wild Pacific coast—a special way to end a day-trip.

---

**Eric Sanford, Liberty Bell Alpine Tours, Mazama, WA 98833; (509)996-2250.** One-day white-water trips through the Black Canyon of the Methow River and 2-hour scenic raft trips in the Methow Valley in summer. Custom trips also available. Cost: $35 for 1-day trips, $10 for 2-hour trips. (TA)

**North Cascades River Expeditions, P.O. Box 116, Arlington, WA 98223; (206) 629-4374.** Day-trips on the Wenatchee, Skagit, and Suiattle rivers. Riverside lunch included. Cost: $35 for Wenatchee trips, $30 for Skagit and Suiattle trips.

**The Northern Wilderness Company, P.O. Box 25795, Seattle, WA 98125; (206) 633-3946.** One-day and moonlight trips on the Skykomish, Wenatchee, Suiattle, Sauk, and Skagit rivers and 1-day trips on the Queets, April through July. Two-day white-water training sessions also available year-round. Cost: $40 for 1-day trips, $35 for moonlight trips, $65 for white-water training.

**Olympic Adventures Inc., P.O. Box 2135, Forks, WA 98331; (206)374-2237.** One-day scenic trips on rain-forest rivers in summer; guides share knowledge of river environs, including geology, natural history, flora and fauna. Cost: $30.

**James Moore or Michael Bellert, ORION Expeditions, Inc., 521 N. 72nd, Seattle, WA 98103; (206)782-8928.** One- and 2-day white-water and scenic trips, April through September, with a close-knit, family atmosphere. Cost: $42 for 1-day trips, $120 for 2-day trips. (TA)

**Jeff Utz, Outdoor Adventures, Box 500,**

Gold Bar, WA 98251; (206)282-8887 or 793-1166. One-day white-water trips on the Skykomish, Wenatchee, and Sauk rivers and 2-day trips including both the Sauk and Suiattle, April through August. Scenic day-trips also offered on the Wenatchee, Skagit, and Queets rivers. Cost: $35 for 1-day trips, $100 for 2-day trips, $12-38 for scenic trips.

David E. Button, Pacific Northwest Float Trips, 829 Waldron St., Sedro Woolley, WA 98204; (206)855-0535. One- and 2-day trips on the Sauk and Suiattle rivers year-round, 1-day trips on the Wenatchee from April through July, and 1-day trips from December through March on the Skagit to observe bald eagles. Cost: $35 for 1-day trips, $100 for 2-day trips, $25 for bald-eagle trips. (TA)

Peter or David Grubb, River Odysseys West, E. 320 17th Ave., Spokane, WA 99203; (509)624-7317. Three-day trips on the Wenatchee River from June through September. Cost: $135. (TA)

Carol Hotz or Ole Hougen, Rivers Northwest, 141 Eagle Ave. N.E., Winslow, WA 98110; (206)842-5144. One-day scenic floats on the Queets, Hoh, and Quinault rivers in summer; winter trips by special arrangement. One-day charter trips on the Wenatchee also available for a minimum of 6 persons. Cost: $40 for Queets, Hoh, and Quinault trips; $57 for Wenatchee trips. (TA)

Jim Fielder, Zig Zag River Runners, Terminal Sales Bldg., 1932 1st Ave., suite 403, Seattle, WA 98101; (206)382-0900. One-day trips on the Skykomish, Wenatchee, Suiattle, and Skagit rivers, April through October; 1-day trips on the Skagit on winter weekends to watch bald eagles; 1-day scenic trips on the Queets, spring through fall. Cost: $42 for Skykomish, Wenatchee, Suiattle, and Queets trips; $27 for regular Skagit trips; $40 for Skagit bald-eagle trips. (TA)

# Oregon

Oregon, like Washington, is divided by the Cascade Mountains into two distinct parts—the damp, forested west and the drier, more sparsely vegetated and populated east. Its rivers, too, reflect this division, from the woodsy white water of the Rogue, Illinois, and Umpqua in the southwestern part of the state to the desertlike runs on the Owyhee and Grande Ronde in the east. In between the two regions, the John Day and Deschutes, tributaries of the Columbia, flow northward out of the state's central valley.

Most famous of Oregon's rivers is the Rogue, one of the original seven "wild" members of the National Wild and Scenic Rivers System. Rapids range from the pulse-quickening kind to the heart-stopping, including the often unrunnable Rainie Falls. The Rogue's tributary, the Illinois, careens down an even narrower and more beautiful canyon in Class IV and V drops, but it can be run for only a few short weeks during spring run-off. Deer, bear, and ospreys are not uncommon in this part of the state and might well be seen on overnight trips on the Rogue or Illinois. The crystal-clear Umpqua northeast of Roseburg is more rarely run, but its thirty-mile course through forests of cedar and Class III-plus white water earns it its Indian name, which means "to satisfy."

The Owyhee River, a tributary of the Snake, flows through a region of colorful volcanic mesas. This heavily canyoned area in southeastern Oregon is so remote that much of it has been explored only by boat. The fact that the Owyhee is the state's least-traveled river makes its forty-mile, Class III run even more attractive. Mink, otter, and beaver are found in the river, pronghorn antelope can be seen along the canyon rim, and golden eagles often are spotted soaring overhead.

In northeastern Oregon, the Grande Ronde (pronounced by the locals more like "ground round" than the French original) spills out of the Wallowa Mountains to begin its journey to the Snake River in Washington. On the way, it courses through lush forests, meadows dusted with wildflowers, and a lunar landscape of lava columns, as well as narrow gorges where it becomes white water. Photographs of this area can be exceptional. Two tributaries of the Grande Ronde, the Wallowa and the Minam, can also be run as an extension of a Grande Ronde trip or on their own. Spring snow melt swells the Minam's eighty-mile length, south of the Grande Ronde, into a white-water run through the rugged Wallowa Mountains. Just to the east of the Minam, the Wallowa's swift currents add excitement and fine fishing to a float down to its confluence with the Grande Ronde.

Other Oregon runs include the Deschutes River, originating in Bend and flowing northward along the eastern edge of the Cascades to its confluence with the Columbia near The Dalles. The river's deep basaltic canyons and the desert landscape of sage, juniper, and cedar are usually hot during rafting season, but the river's cool waters shelter steelhead and swimmers alike. The run also includes a single Class IV rapids some two miles long—Whitehorse, perhaps the most demanding in the West. Somewhat more peaceful is the John Day farther east. In its fascinating canyon, fossils and leaf imprints are found in shale and layers of volcanic rock are clearly defined. Indian petroglyphs, eagles' nests, and Class III white water round out this river's appeal.

---

**Adrift Adventures, Inc., P.O. Box 577, Dept. N., Glenwood Springs, CO 81601;** (303)945-2281. Trips on the Owyhee and Grande Ronde rivers. Cost: available upon request. (TA)

**Stephen L. Cutright, American River Touring Assoc., 1307 Harrison St., Oakland, CA 94612;** (415)465-9355. Three- and 4-day trips on the Rogue River in summer, 4-day trips on the Illinois and 5-day trips on the Owyhee in April and May, and 5-day trips on the Grande Ronde in May and June. Three-day Rogue trip features lodge accommodations. Cost: $235-385.

**Ray Baker, Ray Baker's White Water Guide Service, 88664 Faulhaber Rd., Elmira, OR 97437;** (503)935-3688. Two- or 3-day trips on the Deschutes River and 1-day trips on the McKenzie in summer. Either rafts or drift boats can be used. Cost: $130-200 for Deschutes trips, $30-60 for McKenzie trips. (TA)

**ECHO: The Wilderness Company, Inc., 6505 Telegraph Ave., Oakland, CA 94609;** (415)658-5075. Five-day trips on the Rogue River in August and September and on the Owyhee in May and June. Cost: $295 for Rogue trips, $391 for Owyhee trips. (TA)

**Gary Lane, Eclipse Expeditions, Rt. 1, Cove, OR 97824;** (503)568-4663. Five-day trips on the Grande Ronde in spring; 4-, 6-, and 10-day trips on the Owyhee in May; 5-day fly-in trip on the Minam in June. Winter bald-eagle excursion also offered, as well as a 7-day combination float/horseback trip along the Grande Ronde in June. Cost: $90/day.

**Dave Helfrich River Outfitter, Inc., 47555 McKenzie Hwy., Vida, OR 97488;** (503)

896-3786. Four-day lodge trips on the Rogue River, September through November, using drift boats; 5-day camping trips on the Owyhee in April and May; scenic day-trips on the McKenzie from April through October. Trips on other rivers available by special arrangement. Cost: $540 for Rogue trips, $440-660 for Owyhee trips, $33 for McKenzie trips. (TA)

**Doris Zanelli, Hells Canyon Navigation Co., P.O. Box 145, Oxbow, OR 97840; (503)785-3352.** Six-day trips on the Owyhee River in April and May. Cost: $429. (TA)

**Jerry Hughes or Carole Finley, Hughes River Expeditions, P.O. Box 217, Cambridge, ID 83610; (208)257-3477.** Four- and 6-day expeditions on the Owyhee River in April and May, and 4-day trips encompassing the Grande Ronde and Wallowa rivers from April through June. Longer custom trips also available. Cost: $415-600 for 4-day Owyhee trips, $560 for 6-day trips, $415 for 4-day Grande Ronde/Wallowa trips.

**Hank or Sharon Miller, Idaho Adventures, P.O. Box 834, Salmon, ID 83467; (208)756-2986.** Five-day trips on the Owyhee River in April and May. Cost: $435.

**James Katz, James Henry River Journeys, P.O. Box 708, Stinson Beach, CA 94970; (415)525-6578 or 868-1836.** Six-day trip on the Owyhee River in May and 5-day trips on the Rogue in June. All trips feature participatory paddling and some focus on natural history with a naturalist guide. Cost: $55-70/day. (TA)

**Jan Henderson or Stew Morton, Lute Jerstad Adventures, P.O. Box 19527, Portland, OR 97219; (503)244-4364.** Three- to 5-day trips on the Deschutes, Owyhee, Grande Ronde, John Day, and Rogue rivers, April through September. Guests row 12-foot rafts themselves. Ten-day itinerary including visits to 2 resorts also available. Cost: $260 for 3-day trips, $430-485 for 5-day trips. (TA)

**Martin Litton, Martin Litton's Grand Canyon Dories, P.O. Box 3029, Stanford, CA 94305; (415)851-0411.** Five-day trips on the Owyhee River in May and 5- and 7-day trips on the Grande Ronde in May and June. Nature study and photography emphasized. Cost: $300 for 5-day trips, $450 for 7-day trips. (TA)

**Vic McLean, Vic McLean's Wildriver Tours, P.O. Box 500, Lotus, CA 95651; (916)626-5042.** Four-day trips on the Rogue River in June and July, 5-day on the Grande Ronde in May and June and on the Deschutes in July, and 6-day trips on the Owyhee in April and May. Custom trips also available. Cost: $260.

**Northwest Outward Bound School, 0110 S.W. Bancroft, Portland, OR 97201; (503)243-1993.** Eight-day trips on the Deschutes River in July and August emphasizing personal and social growth. Cost: $400.

**Galand Haas, Northwest Whitewater Excursions, P.O. Box 10754, Eugene, OR 97440; (503)266-2974.** Five-day trips on the Owyhee River, April through June; and 2-, 3-, and 4-day trips on the Deschutes, July through September. One- to 4-day trips on the McKenzie, John Day, Wallowa, and Grande Ronde also offered. Cost: $430 for Owyhee trips, $195 for 2-day Deschutes trips, $270 for 3-day Deschutes trips, $55-365 for other trips. (TA)

**Robert Doppelt, Oregon River Experiences, 1935 Hayes St., Eugene, OR 97405; (503)342-3293.** Row-it-yourself white-water trips: 4-day trips on the Owyhee River in May, 3-day trips on the Deschutes from June through August, 2-day trips on the Umpqua in June, 3-day trips on the Rogue in September. Cost: $188 for Owyhee trips, $168 for Deschutes trips, $72 for Umpqua trips, $186 for Rogue trips.

**Anna M. Alden, Osprey River Trips, Inc., 6109 Fish Hatchery Rd., Grants Pass, OR 97526; (503)479-4215.** Three-, 4-, and 5-day trips on the Rogue River, April through September. Natural history tours, white-water guide school, workshops for women, and family trips also offered. Trips feature relaxed pace and gourmet food. Cost: $180-350. (TA)

John or Sharon Vail, Outdoors Unlimited River Trips, P.O. Box 22513, Sacramento, CA 95822; (916)452-1081. Five-day trips on the Rogue River in summer. Cost: $339. (TA)

Gary Rhinehart, Rhinehart's Guide Service, 5649 McLoughlin Dr., Central Point, OR 97502; (503)779-1880. Three- and 4-day camping or lodge trips on the Rogue River from June through September. One-day excursions on the upper Rogue available from May through November. Cost: $230 for 3-day trips, $280 for 4-day trips.

Peter or David Grubb, River Odysseys West, E. 320 17th Ave., Spokane, WA 99203; (509)624-7317. Five-day trips and 6-day white-water school on the Owyhee River, March through June; 5-day trips on the Grande Ronde, May through July, and on the Rogue in September and October; 6-day trips on the John Day, April through July. Some trips focus on wilderness appreciation or learning white-water skills. Cost: $240-340.

Irvine L. Urie, River Trips Unlimited, 900 Murphy Rd., Medford, OR 97501; (503) 779-3798. Three- and 4-day trips on the Rogue River in summer with accommodations in lodges along the river. Cost: $250 for 3-day trips, $325 for 4-day trips.

Carol Hotz or Ole Hougen, Rivers Northwest, 141 Eagle Ave., N.E., Winslow, WA 98110; (206)842-5144. One- and 3-day trips on the Deschutes Rives, May through October, and 5-day trips on the Owyhee, March through June. Cost: $53 for 1-day trips, $207 for 3-day trips, $360 for 5-day trips. (TA)

Ken Robertson and Sons Guide Service, 3424 Amber Lane, Grants Pass, OR 97526; (503)479-9554. Three-day trips on the Rogue River in summer and 5-day trips on the Owyhee in May and June.

Cost: $200 for 3-day trips. (TA)

Bob or Jan Sevy, Sevy Guide Service, Box 1527, Sun Valley, ID 83353; (208)788-3440. Five- and 7-day trips on the Owyhee River in April and May featuring specialized service tailored to groups' needs. Cost: $100/day.

Outing Dept., Sierra Club, 530 Bush St., San Francisco, CA 94108; (415)981-8634. Five-day trips on the Rogue River in summer. Cost: $355.

Michael R. Saul, Sundance Expeditions Inc., 14894 Galice Rd., Merlin, OR 97532; (503)479-8508. Four-day trips on the Illinois River in April and May; 4- and 5-day trips on the Rogue from June through September, including some lodge trips. Professional white-water school also offered. Cost: $330 for Illinois trips, $275 for 4-day Rogue trips, $325 for 5-day trips, $415 for lodge trips. (TA)

Ted Birdseye, Sunrise Scenic Tours, 3791 Rogue River Hwy., Gold Hill, OR 97525; (503)582-0202. One- to 5-day trips on the Rogue, Umpqua, and Deschutes rivers from May through September; 4-day Illinois trips in May and June. Both rafts and inflatable kayaks are used. Cost: $35 for 1-day trips, $135 for 2-day trips, $185 for 3-day trips, $265 for 4-day trips, $295 for 5-day trips. (TA)

Jim or Toni Walker, Walker River Expeditions, Rt. 1, Box 228-F, Enterprise, OR 97828; (503)426-3307. Four-day trips on the Owyhee River in May and 3-day trips on the Grande Ronde in June. Owyhee trips include a plane ride back over the river canyon to the trip's starting point. Cost: $339 for Owyhee trips, $249 for Grande Ronde trips.

Ken Warren, Ken Warren Outdoors, 9100 S.E. 92nd, Portland, OR 97266; (503) 777-1828 or 254-3245 or 638-4327. Four-, 5-, and 7-day trips on the Owyhee River; 5-day trips on the Rogue; 3-day trips on the Grande Ronde, Deschutes, or John Day. Trips offered from April through September. Six-day combination float/

horseback trip on the Grande Ronde and into Wenaha River country also available, May through July. Cost: $235 for 3-day trips, $375 for 4-day trips, $445 for 5-day trips, $595 for 7-day trips or float/horseback trips. (TA)

**Muriel Whitmore, Bryce Whitmore Wilderness Water Ways, 33 Canyon Dr., Port Costa, CA 94569; (415)787-2820 or (503) 479-2021.** Four-day camping trips on the Illinois River from April through June, and 3-day lodge or camping trips on the Rogue in summer. Paddle rafts or inflatable kayaks available by special arrangement. Cost: $250 for Illinois trips, $160 for Rogue camping trips, $180 for lodge trips.

**Tom Malcamp or Bonnie Maler, Wilderland, 930 Irving St., San Francisco, CA 94122; (415)504-7513.** Four-day trips on the Grande Ronde River in July and 6-day trips on the Owyhee in May. Inflatable kayaks available on most trips. Cost: $310 for Grande Ronde trips, $350 for Owyhee trips. (TA)

**The Tonsmeires, Wilderness River Outfitters and Trail Expeditions, Inc., P.O. Box 871, Salmon, ID 83467; (208)756-3959.**
Five- to 17-day expeditions on the Owyhee River in April and May. Cost: $325-1600. (TA)

**Nada Kovalik, Wilderness World, 1342 Jewell Ave., Pacific Grove, CA 93950; (408)373-5882.** Trips on the Owyhee and Umpqua rivers in May and on the Rogue throughout the summer. Paddle-boat option available on Rogue and Owyhee trips. Cost: $300 for Rogue and Owyhee trips, $240 for Umpqua trips. (TA)

**Richard or Rochelle Wright, Wright's River Explorations, 549 Ioco Rd., Port Moody, B.C., Canada V3H 2W3; (604) 461-6361.** Four-day trips on the Rogue River, July through October. Inflatable kayaks available. Cost: $250(U.S.).

# Idaho

Commercial rafting in Idaho has reached a level of professionalism matched only in Arizona's Grand Canyon. Companies are licensed by the

state, user days are limited on some rivers, and guides must be certified graduates of intensive training programs for each river they run. This virtually ensures you of having an informative, well-run trip, and you'll be grateful for it when you see the white water in Hells Canyon on the Snake River or venture down the Salmon, the "River of No Return."

The Snake separates Oregon from Idaho by cutting the deepest river gorge in North America, Hells Canyon. For a fifteen-mile stretch, the canyon's average depth is 6,600 feet, with an extreme of 7,900 feet. It is also the narrowest gorge on the continent, and the combination of vertical basaltic walls and Class V white water for trips up to a week long is too intimidating for some. Even though much of the river has been mellowed by the Hells Canyon Dam, the fifteen-foot waves in the famous rapids at Wild Sheep and Granite Creek are not to be missed if you like white water. Petroglyphs from long-forgotten peoples, stone shelters and caves, abandoned mines, and weathered cabins lend historical interest, while working ranches and an occasional jet boat making a speedy one-day trip are reminders of the world outside. The upper Snake is the site of a float through the Birds of Prey Natural Area, where fourteen species of raptors—including the rare peregrine falcon—soar through the Snake River Canyon.

The Main Fork of the Salmon River cuts the continent's second deepest canyon (the Grand Canyon is but the third deepest) as it flows through Idaho's vast Primitive Area. Lewis and Clark heeded the advice of the Nez Perce Indians living nearby and looked elsewhere for their navigable waterway to the Pacific. It's a good thing they did—the "River of No Return" has treacherous Class V rapids, like Bailey and Whiplash, set amidst a rugged country. The Salmon's Middle Fork is only a little less intimidating, with its Class IV white water found in places with names like Impassable Canyon. Salmon, steelhead, and trout make this stretch a favorite with fishermen; black bear, eagles, elk, and bighorn sheep attract wildlife enthusiasts; and heavily forested slopes, stands of ponderosa pine in granite canyons, and sunny summer weather make it a photographer's paradise.

The other major Idaho river trip is on the Selway, from the Bitterroot Range near the Idaho-Montana border down to Selway Falls in the wilderness area. Elk, moose, mountain goats, and bighorn sheep may be sighted, and the majestic mountain panoramas and forested steep canyons provide a perfect wild setting. Its Class IV to V white water is recommended for experienced rafters, and children are not encouraged to participate. The Jarbridge and Bruneau rivers in southern Idaho also are rafted for seventy-five miles of Class III and IV small-stream white water, on a five-day run limited to four guests—one per boat.

---

**Adrift Adventures, Inc., P.O. Box 577, Dept. N., Glenwood Springs, CO 81601; (303)945-2281.** Raft trips on the Main Salmon River. Cost: available upon request. (TA)

**Stephen L. Cutright, American River Touring Assoc., 1307 Harrison St., Oakland, CA 94612; (415)465-9355.** Five- and 6-day trips on the Main Salmon River, 6-day trips on the Middle Fork of the Salmon and on the Snake, and 5-day trips on the Selway in summer. Many trips offer paddle-raft option. Cost: $400 for 5-day Main Salmon trips, $425 for 6-day Main Salmon trips, $520 for Middle Fork and Snake trips, $565 for Selway trips.

**ECHO: The Wilderness Company, Inc., 6505 Telegraph Ave., Oakland, CA 94609; (415)658-5075.** Six-day trips through Hells Canyon of the Snake River, on the Main Salmon, or on the Middle Fork in summer. Five-day trips on the lower Main Salmon in September and 3-day bird-watching trips in the Snake River's Birds of Prey Natural Area in May also offered. Cost: $480-515 for Hells Canyon and Main Salmon trips, $540-595 for Middle Fork trips, $365 for lower Salmon trips, $235 for Birds of Prey trips. (TA)

Woodrow M. Hassinger, Frontier Expeditions, Inc., Box 839, N. Fork, ID 83466; (208)865-2200 or (303)693-0349. Five-day trips on the Main Salmon River or the Middle Fork in summer. Cost: $585 for Main Salmon trips, $625 for Middle Fork trips. (TA)

Norm or Bill Guth, Box D, Salmon, ID 83467; (208)756-3279. Five-day trips on the Main Salmon River or the Middle Fork in summer. Alternative 5-day trips on the Main Salmon include jet-boat ride back up the river to starting point. Cost: $450 for Main Salmon trips, $500 for Middle Fork trips.

Don Hatch, Don Hatch River Expeditions, Inc., P.O. Box C, Vernal, UT 84078; (801)789-4316 or 4715. Five-day trips on the Middle Fork of the Salmon River and on the Selway in summer offered by company that pioneered river rafting in Idaho. Cost: $530 for Middle Fork trips, $650 for Selway trips. (TA)

Doris Zanelli, Hells Canyon Navigation Co., P.O. Box 145, Oxbow, OR 97840; (503)785-3352. Six-day float trips through Hells Canyon in summer. Inflatable kayaks available. Six-day combination float/ horseback trip in Hells Canyon and the Wallowa Mountains also offered in June and August. Cost: $429. (TA)

Dave Helfrich River Outfitter, Inc., 47555 McKenzie Hwy., Vida, OR 97488; (503) 896-3786. Five-day trips on the lower Main Salmon River in August and 6-day trips on the Middle Fork from June to August. Cost: $440 for lower Salmon trips; $660-935 for Middle Fork trips. (TA)

Dee or Sue Holladay, Holiday River Expeditions, 519 Malibu Dr., Salt Lake City, UT 84107; (801)266-2087. Six-day trips on the Main Salmon River and 3-day trips on the lower Main Salmon offered from May through September. Six-day trip includes scenic flight from McCall back to Salmon, Idaho. Cost: $490 for 6-day trips, $210 for 3-day trips. (TA)

Jerry Hughes or Carole Finley, Hughes

River Expeditions, P.O. Box 217, Cambridge, ID 83610; (208)257-3477. Four- and 6-day expeditions through Hells Canyon, on the Main Salmon River, or on the lower Main Salmon, and 6-day trips on the Middle Fork offered from May through October. Special wildlife-spotting and photography trips and combination float/backpack trips also available. Cost: $415-500 for 4-day trips, $560-580 for 6-day trips.

Hank or Sharon Miller, Idaho Adventures, P.O. Box 834, Salmon, ID 83467; (208)756-2986. Six-day trips on the Main Salmon River or the Middle Fork from spring through fall or on the Snake in summer. Spring trips often focus on photography. Five-day trips on the lower Main Salmon and the Snake also available in September and October. Cost: $515 for Main Salmon and Snake trips, $550 for Middle Fork trips, $435 for lower-Salmon/Snake trips.

Jan Henderson or Stew Morton, Lute Jerstad Adventures, P.O. Box 19527, Portland, OR 97219; (503)244-4364. Five-day trips on the Snake River, including Hells Canyon, from May through September. Guests can row their own 12-foot rafts. Cost: $430-485. (TA)

Martin Litton, Martin Litton's Grand Canyon Dories, P.O. Box 3029, Stanford, CA 94305; (415)851-0411. Seven-day lodge trips on the Main Salmon River in May and July; 8-day camping trips on the Main Salmon from May through September; 5-day trips on the lower Main Salmon and through Hells Canyon from July through September; 13-day trips encompassing both the 8- and 5-day itineraries from July through September; and 6-day trips through Hells Canyon from May through October. Cost: $368-860. (TA)

Joan Kuebler, Mackay Bar Corp., 3190 Airport Way, Boise, ID 83705; (208) 344-1881. Six-day trips on the Main Salmon River or the Middle Fork, and 5-day trips on the Main Salmon that include 1 day at ranch offering horseback riding, fishing, and jet-boating. Four- and

6-day combination float/horseback/ ranch trips and 3-day float trip in the Birds of Prey Natural Area also offered. Trips scheduled throughout the summer except Birds of Prey trip, which is in May. Cost: $400 for 3-day trip, $565 for 4-day trips, $715 for 5-day trips, $680 for 6-day Main Salmon trips, $720 for Middle Fork trips, $815 for 6-day combination trips.(TA)

**Ken Masoner, Ken Masoner's Custom River Tours, Box 184, Twin Falls, ID 83301; (208)733-4548.** Six-day trips on the Middle Fork of the Salmon River offered in summer, and at other times by special arrangement. Cost: $551.

**Nick Nicholson, Nicholson and Sons Float Trips Inc., Rt. 4, Box 113, Twin Falls, ID 83301; (208)733-6139 or 774-3528.** Six-day trips on the Middle Fork of the Salmon River in summer. Shorter fly-in trips also available upon request. Cost: $495. (TA)

**Galand Haas, Northwest Whitewater Excursions, P.O. Box 10754, Eugene, OR 97440; (503)266-2974.** Five-day trips on the Main Salmon River and through Hells Canyon, July through September. Cost: $430. (TA)

**Robert Doppelt, Oregon River Experiences, 1935 Hayes St., Eugene, OR 97405; (503)342-3293.** Five-day row-it-yourself trips on the lower Main Salmon River in July and August. Cost: $264.

**Bob Volpert, Outdoor Adventures Inc., 3109 Fillmore St., San Francisco, CA 94123; (415)346-8700.** Six-day trips on the Main Salmon River or Middle Fork and 12-day trips combining the two. Six-day trips also offered on the Snake. Trips offered from May to September. Cost: $660 for Salmon or Middle Fork trips, $1,045 for 12-day combination trips, $534 for Snake trips. (TA)

**David or Sheila Mills, Rocky Mountain River Tours, P.O. Box 693, Pocatello, ID 83201; (208)232-7064.** Five-day trips on the lower Main Salmon River, 4½- and 6-

day trips on the Main Salmon, and 3-day trips through Hells Canyon from April through October; 6-day trips on the Middle Fork from June to September. One- or 2-day trips in the Birds of Prey Natural Area available upon request. Cost: $530 for lower Salmon and 4½-day Main Salmon trips, $615 for 6-day Main Salmon trips, $410 for Hells Canyon trips, $665 for Middle Fork trips.

**Stephen Dixon, Salmon River Lodge, Inc., P.O. Box 348, Jerome, ID 83338; (208)324-3553 or 5568.** One-, 2-, 4-, and 5-day trips on the Main Salmon River in summer. Four-day trips include jet-boat ride back to starting point. Ten-day combination float/horseback trips also offered. Cost: $475 for 4-day trips. (TA)

**Bob or Jan Sevy, Sevy Guide Service, Box 1527, Sun Valley, ID 83353; (208)788-3440.** Six-day trips on the Main Salmon River or the Middle Fork, June to September; 5-day trips on the lower Main Salmon by arrangement, April to October; 4-day trips in Hells Canyon, May to October. Cost: $600 for Main Salmon trips, $650 for Middle Fork trips, $500 for lower Salmon trips, $425 for Hells Canyon trips.

**Outing Dept., Sierra Club, 530 Bush St., San Francisco, CA 94108; (415)981-8634.** Eight-day trip on the Main Salmon River and 6-day trip in Hells Canyon in summer. Inflatable kayaks available. Cost: $645 for Main Salmon trip, $485 for Hells Canyon trip.

**Ken Smith, Ken Smith's Middle Fork River Expeditions, P.O. Box 779, N. Fork, ID 83466; (208)865-2498.** Five-day trips on the Middle Fork of the Salmon River from June through September. Private trips for individual parties or composite trips are available. Cost: $475. (TA)

**Glen R. Foster, Teton Expeditions, Inc., P.O. Box 218, Rigby, ID 83442; (208)523-4981 or 745-6476.** Six-day trips on the Main Salmon River and 5-day trips on the Middle Fork or lower Main Salmon in summer. Cost: $515 for Main Salmon trips, $455 for Middle Fork trips, $425 for lower Salmon trips. (TA)

**Jim or Toni Walker, Walker River Expeditions, Rt. 1, Box 228-F, Enterprise, OR 97828; (503)426-3307.** Three- to 5-day trips in Hells Canyon from May to September; 5-day trips on the Main Salmon River from July to September. Inflatable kayaks available. Cost: $289 for 3-day trips, $339 for 4-day trips, $429 for 5-day Hells Canyon trips, $469 for Main Salmon trips.

**Ken Warren, Ken Warren Outdoors, 9100 S.E. 92nd, Portland, OR 97266; (503) 777-1828 or 254-3245 or 638-4327.** Five-day raft trips and 8-day combination raft/horseback trips in Hells Canyon from May to September; 5-day raft trips on the lower Main Salmon in summer. Cost: $445 for 5-day trips, $795 for 8-day trips. (TA)

**John Jones, Whitewater River Tours, N.W. 720 Gary St., Pullman, WA 99163; (509)332-4862.** Three-, 4-, and 5-day trips on the lower Main Salmon River and the Snake, on the upper Main Salmon, and in Hells Canyon, May through October. Cost: available upon request.

**Carl Russell, Jr., Wilderness Encounters, Inc., 693 W. Grand River, Okemas, MI 48864; (517)349-5042.** Six-day trips on the Middle Fork of the Salmon River, June through August; 4- and 6-day trips in Hells Canyon, May through September; and 5-day trips on the lower Main Salmon, July through September. Cost: $395 for 4-day trips, $495 for 5-day trips, $595 for 6-day trips.

**The Tonsmeires, Wilderness River Outfitters and Trail Expeditions, Inc., P.O. Box 871, Salmon, ID 83467; (208)756-3959.** Four-day trips on the Main Salmon River, April through October, and in Hells Canyon, May through September; 5-day trips on the Bruneau River. Bruneau trips have 1-to-1 guest-to-guide ratio and include scenic flight to put-in point. Seven-day combination backpack/float trip in Seven Devils Mountains and Hells Canyon also

offered. Cost: $600 for Main Salmon and backpack/float trips, $450 for Hells Canyon trips, $720 for Bruneau trips. (TA)

**Richard Jones, World Wide Expeditions, Inc., 175 E. 7060 S., Midvale, UT 84047; (801)566-2662.** Six-day trips on the Main Salmon River in summer, either in rafts or in row-your-own sportyaks. Cost: $425. (TA)

**Robert Ferguson, Zephyr River Expeditions, P.O. Box 2607, Sonora, CA 95370; (209)532-6249.** Six-day trips on the Main Salmon River or the Middle Fork and 12-day trips combining the two in summer. Cost: $600 for 6-day trips, $950 for 12-day trips. (TA)

# California

Northern California's rivers can be divided into two major groups. The first is the more northern, flowing out of the Siskiyou Mountains that border Oregon, west to the Pacific. This group includes the Klamath, Salmon, Eel, and Trinity rivers. The rivers of the second group—the American, Tuolumne, Stanislaus, Sacramento, Merced, and Carson—all have their headwaters in the Sierra Nevada. This latter group is somewhat different in mood from other Northwest rivers, being on the whole hotter, drier, and more crowded. But all of them are within a half day's drive of San Francisco and are north of Monterey Bay, thereby fitting into the regions included in this book.

These Sierra Nevada rivers provide some of the best combinations of white water and warm weather in the country. The Tuolumne is almost in a class by itself, a seventeen-mile run that courses through sheer canyons and features more than one Class V rapids. The American and Stanislaus are both a bit less technical but have rapids thrilling enough to bear such names as Widowmaker, Death Rock, and Meatgrinder. The Merced is located just outside of Yosemite National Park, which virtually ensures its scenic value, with nineteenth-century railroad trestles and a twenty-foot waterfall adding to its attractions. Only the Carson flows east from the Sierra Nevada—and the East Fork Carson is as good an introduction to rafting as any, running through polished granite canyons, past pine and cottonwood stands and a mineral hot springs, and into the Nevada desert. Trips on these rivers range from one to three days in duration, limited by the profusion of hydroelectric projects. From Redding, the Sacramento River also offers two one-day floats—either peaceful nature floats on the lower section of the river or stimulating white-water trips through the canyons above Lake Shasta, where the river drops an average of forty-five feet per mile.

The Klamath River and its tributaries provide a much different river experience. The Klamath actually begins in Oregon, but its Class III and IV white water is in California's Siskiyou Mountains. The pine forests support rich populations of deer, bear, otter, bald eagles, blue herons, and ospreys, while salmon and steelhead run in the river itself. Bigfoot, the North-west's legendary creature that defies explanation as well as the one at Loch Ness, also is rumored to be around here, so bring your camera and lots of credibility. The Trinity has several raftable stretches, which vary in degree of difficulty and can be toured either in one-day trips or all at once on a three- or four-day venture. The Salmon is one of the least rafted of California rivers, due at least in part to its wild course: it drops an average of sixty-six feet per mile, compared with thirty-four feet on the rugged Tuolumne. Only oared two-day trips are available on this one, and customers are required to wear wet suits and have previous white-water experience.

Finally, one- to three-day floats are available on the Middle Fork of the Eel, which has the longest stretch of wilderness river left in the state. No roads run beside or even to the river for the thirty river miles of the trip, which rides Class III rapids through fir forests and canyons of idyllic beauty.

---

**George Armstrong, All-Outdoors Adventure Trips, 2151 San Miguel Dr., Walnut**

Creek, CA 94596; (415)934-0240. One- and 2-day trips on the American and Stanislaus rivers, April through October, and on the Merced, April through July; 2- or 3-day trips on the Klamath, June through August; 2-day trips on the East Fork Carson in May and June; 3-day trips on the Eel in May. Seven-day float/ backpack trips offered for teens in summer. Cost: $50/day. (TA)

**Stephen L. Cutright, American River Touring Assoc., 1307 Harrison St., Oakland, CA 94612; (415)465-9355.** One- to 7-day trips on the American, Stanislaus, Tuolumne, Eel, and Merced rivers, April through September. Many trips have paddle-raft option and some are lodge trips. Cost: $53 for 1-day trips, $350 for 5-day trips.

**Roy or Jeane Frostrom, Cool River Rafts, 6017 Troy Lane, Palo Cedro, CA 96073; (916)547-4000.** One-day and evening trips on the Sacramento River year-round. Day-trips include restaurant lunch. Cost: $20 for day-trips, $12 for evening trips. (TA)

**ECHO: The Wilderness Company, Inc., 6505 Telegraph Ave., Oakland, CA 94609; (415)658-5075.** One- and 2-day trips on the American and Stanislaus rivers; 2-day trips on the Merced and East Fork Carson; 2-, 3-, and 4-day trips on the Klamath and Tuolumne. American, Stanislaus, and Tuolumne trips are offered from April to October, Merced trips from April to July, East Fork Carson trips from May to July, and Klamath trips from June to August. Cost: $57 for 1-day trips, $109-165 for 2-day trips, $225 for 3-day trips, $265 for 4-day trips. (TA)

**James H. Katz, James Henry River Journeys, P.O. Box 708, Stinson Beach, CA 94970; (415)525-6578 or 868-1836.** One- and 2-day trips on the Stanislaus, American, and Merced rivers; 2-day trips on the East Fork Carson; 4-day trips on the Klamath; and 1- to 3-day trips on the Eel. Season is from April to September. White-water workshops on the American and Stanislaus also offered. Cost:

$55-70/day. (TA)

**Vic McLean, Vic McLean's Wildriver Tours, P.O. Box 500, Lotus, CA 95651; (916)626-5042.** One- and 2-day trips on the American and Stanislaus rivers from April through October, 2-day trips on the Merced and East Fork Carson from April through July, and 2-day or longer trips on the Eel from April through June and on the Klamath from April through October. Cost: $48-62 for 1-day trips, $98-125 for 2-day trips.

**Anna M. Alden, Osprey River Trips, Inc., 6109 Fish Hatchery Rd., Grants Pass, OR 97526; (503)479-4215.** Three- and 4-day trips on the Klamath River in summer. Inflatable kayaks and paddle boats available. Natural history tours, workshops for women, and family trips also offered. Cost: $180-250. (TA)

**Bob Volpert, Outdoor Adventures Inc., 3109 Fillmore St., San Francisco, CA 94123; (415)346-8700.** One- and 2-day trips on the American and Stanislaus rivers from April through October, 2-day trips on the Merced from April through July and on the East Fork Carson in May and June, and 2- and 3-day trips on the Tuolumne from March through October. Cost: $55-66 for 1-day trips, $110-182 for 2-day trips, $248 for 3-day trips. (TA)

**John or Sharon Vail, Outdoors Unlimited River Trips, P.O. Box 22513, Sacramento, CA 95822; (916)452-1081.** Two-day trips on the Merced in spring, 2- and 3-day trips on the Tuolumne from March to September, and 3- and 6-day trips on the Klamath in summer. Cost: $150 for Merced trips, $200 for 2-day Tuolumne trips, $270 for 3-day Tuolumne trips, $200 for 3-day Klamath trips, $350 for 6-day trips. (TA)

**Shane or Sundra Murphy, Sandpiper Whitewater Guides, Box 11752, Zephyr Cove, NV 89448; (702)588-4074.** Weekend trips on the Eel River in April and May, 3-day trips on the Klamath in summer, and ½-day and 2-day trips on the American from April to October. White-water school also offered on the American and Eel. Cost: $103 for Eel trips, $167 for Klamath trips, $33-45 for ½-day American trips, $100 for 2-day American trips. (TA)

**Timothy Menasco, Sierra Western River Guides, P.O. Box 2135, Placerville, CA 95667; (800)453-1482 (toll free).** One- and 2-day trips on the American River, May through September. Paddle-boat option available. Company uses its own private 27-acre camp. Cost: $40 for 1-day trips, $100 for 2-day trips. (TA)

**Ted Birdseye, Sunrise Scenic Tours, 3791 Rogue River Hwy., Gold Hill, OR 97525; (503)582-0202.** One- to 5-day trips on the Klamath River from June to September. Both rafts and inflatable kayaks can be used. Cost: $35 for 1-day trips, $135 for 2-day trips, $185 for 3-day trips, $265 for 4-day trips, $295 for 5-day trips. (TA)

**Swede or Carolle Turner, Whitewater High, P.O. Box 670, Big Bar, CA 96010; (916)623-2227.** One- to 4-day trips on the Klamath River from June to October; 1- and 2-day trips on the Salmon and 1- to 3-day trips on the Trinity from March to June. Cost: $30-90 for 1-day trips, $65-150 for 2-day trips, $105-140 for 3-day trips, $170 for 4-day trips.

**Tom Malcamp or Bonnie Maler, Wilderland, 930 Irving St., San Francisco, CA 94122; (415)564-7513.** Two-day trips on the Klamath, East Fork Carson, and American rivers in summer. Cost: $100. (TA)

**Dean Munroe, Wilderness Adventures, Inc., 430 Buckeye Terrace #3, Redding, CA 96001; (916)243-3091.** One-day trips in the upper Sacramento River canyon in spring and early summer and 2-day trips in Hell's Corner Gorge of the Klamath canyon year-round. Company was first outfitter on the upper Sacramento and first ever to run Hell's Corner Gorge, which has 40 major rapids. Cost: $55 for Sacramento trips, $160 for Hell's Corner trips. (TA)

**Paul Parker or Paul Bachinger, Wild River Raftin' Co., P.O. Box 11583, Tahoe Para-** dise, CA 95708; (916)577-5646. One- and 2-day weekend trips on the East Fork Carson River from April to July; 1- and 2-day trips on the American and 3- to 6-day trips on the Klamath from April to September. Custom trips available on the Eel and Trinity. Cost: $37 for 1-day trips, $90 for 2-day trips, $145 for 3-day trips. (TA)

**O.K. or Glenna Goodwin, World of Whitewater, P.O Box 708, Big Bar, CA 96010; (916)623-6588.** One-day trips on the Trinity and Klamath rivers. Cost: $25-35.

**Robert Ferguson, Zephyr River Expeditions, P.O. Box 2607, Sonora, CA 95370; (209)532-6249.** One-, 2-, and 3-day trips on the Stanislaus River; 1- and 2-day trips on the Merced and American; 2-day trips on the East Fork Carson; and 2- and 3-day trips on the Eel. Stanislaus and American trips run from April through October, Eel trips in April and May, and East Fork Carson and Merced trips from April through July. Cost: $50-75 for 1-day trips, $95-115 for 2-day trips, $165 for 3-day trips. (TA)

# SAILING

One of the most popular water sports in the Pacific Northwest, sailing is also a wonderful way to see the many different faces of the region. From the driftwood-strewn beaches beneath virgin forests high up the Inside Passage to the growing skyline of Seattle as approached from Elliott Bay, it is a territory with attractions for everyone. Mild temperatures, consistent winds, and an endless selection of courses to chart have made the waters that lap against the Washington and British Columbia coastlines particularly popular.

In 1792 Captain George Vancouver sailed through the Strait of Juan de Fuca, between the Olympic Peninsula and Vancouver Island, to explore Puget Sound. This mazelike assortment of channels, inlets, islands, and peninsulas still offers some of the best sailing in the world. Marinas large and small, and major ports and long-forgotten docks provide moorage for sailboats of all sizes. The larger of the San Juan Islands, for instance, have fishing villages and resorts, while the smaller ones are uninhabited, providing an idyllic retreat for campers, swimmers, and fishermen who arrive under sail.

British Columbia's Vancouver Island is the largest island on the west coast of the continent, and sailing up its 285-mile length can be an endlessly fascinating trip. Ferries connect the island to the mainland in several places, but there still remains plenty of coastline so remote that you will feel as much a discoverer as the early sailors. Small fishing villages of the Kwakiutl, Bellacoola, and other native Americans still cling to the coast at river mouths. All the way up to Prince Rupert at the head of the Inside Passage, the interface of land and sea provides an incredible array of sights—waterfalls that plunge into the ocean, tall conifers that lean precariously over steep cliffs, snow-topped mountains that kiss the sky just a few miles from the Pacific.

These and other sights can be enjoyed by chartering a sailboat or learning how to sail from an outfitter or school. Bareboat charters include only the boat, usually rented by the week, and perhaps some supplies; skippered charters include a minimal crew, allowing clients either to learn as the cruise progresses or just sit back and enjoy their adventure.

If you elect to learn sailing, then a whole new set of skills must be mastered. You must learn the difference between a sloop and a schooner, a Marconi mainsail and a mizzen staysail; and you must learn how to tie a reef knot to join two ropes and a cleat half-hitch to secure halyards. Tacking will become as second nature as jibbing, and before you know it you'll be broad-reaching with the best of them, slicing across the clear salt waters of the Northwest with a far-off forested isle as your destination.

# British Columbia

Brian McDonald, Black Tusk Touring and Guide Service Ltd., 3064 St. Kildas Ave., N. Vancouver, B.C., Canada V7N 2A9; (604)985-9223. Seven-day Gulf Island cruises, 9-day Inside Passage cruises, and 14-day cruises along Vancouver Island's west coast from March through September, with a new anchorage each day offering opportunity for exploring, dinghy

sailing, swimming, fishing, or relaxing. Cost: $395(U.S.) for 7-day cruises, $625 for 9-day cruises, $1,095 for 14-day cruises.

**Jim or Myrna Boulding, Strathcona Park Lodge and Outdoor Education Centre, Box 2160, Campbell River, B.C., Canada V9W 5C9; Campbell River radio, Strathcona Lodge 59 7021.** Two- and 3-day intensive introductory sailing courses in May, June, and October, emphasizing actual practice; 3-day program includes an overnight camping trip. Seven-day sailing instruction program in July and August encompassing both lake and ocean sailing and offering excellent opportunity to explore the British Columbia coastline. Packages include lodging and meals at the centre, which is located at the edge of a 30-mile lake and overlooks the entry to Strathcona Provincial Park, a rugged mountain wilderness area. Cost: $85 (Cdn.) for 2-day courses, $110 for 3-day courses, $260 for 7-day courses. (TA)

**Dan Culver, Whitewater Adventures Ltd., 105 W. 6th Ave., Vancouver, B.C., Canada V5Y 1K3; (604)879-6701.** Seven- and 9-day cruises from May through October along the coast of British Columbia. Sailboats are 51 feet long, offer comfortable accommodations. Opportunity for fishing, swimming, hiking, and exploring. Cost: $425-750(U.S.). (TA)

# Washington

**Jim Shea or John Dean, Anacortes Yacht Charters, P.O. Box 69, 3005 Commercial Ave., Anacortes, WA 98221; (206) 293-4555.** Sailboats for bareboat charters on a weekly basis to cruise the San Juan and Gulf islands and north to Desolation Sound and Princess Louisa Inlet. Company will fully outfit boat with provisions, bedding, and fishing equipment if desired, and has an "Island Sampler Cruise" itinerary available for those un-

familiar with the area. Sailing lessons and skippered sail-and-learn cruises also offered. Cost: $450-1,300/week.

**Sean or Cheri Riley, Cascade Sailing Cruises, 6863 Eagle Harbor Dr., Bainbridge Island, WA 98110; (206)842-8373.** Five-day instructional cruises through the San Juan Islands, May 1 through October 31. All aspects of sailing are demonstrated; guests can participate in sailing as much or as little as they wish. Guests have free access to facilities at resorts visited. Year-round charters also available. Cost: $450, includes all meals except dinners. (TA)

**Carol Rush, Crew Pool, 106 Central Way, Kirkland, WA 98033; (206)822-4157.** Free year-round referral service for persons wishing to be crew members on sailboats. Basic sailing skill and gear required. Crewing classes also offered. Cost: referral service free, cost of classes available upon request.

**Robert or Ann Dursch, EOS II, 3618 Oakes Ave., Anacortes, WA 98221; (206)293-3044.** Six-day cruises offered from mid-June to early September, with activities planned around guests' interests. Instruction in sailing and racing techniques, oceanography for boaters, and natural history of the area available on board if desired. Cost: $350/person for composite cruise; $1,400 for 4 persons, $1,650 for 5, $1,900 for 6 for 1-party cruises; includes all meals. (TA)

**Knute Mattison, Ocean Services, 4600 Leary Way N.W., Seattle, WA 98107; (206)784-8703.** Skippered or bareboat sailing charters available year-round for cruising in the San Juan Islands and along the coast of British Columbia. Three-day sail-and-learn cruises also offered. Cost: $350-5,000/week. (TA)

**Oceanic Society Expeditions, Bldg. E, Fort Mason Center, San Francisco, CA 94123; (415)441-1106.** Year-round custom and scheduled excursions along the Pacific coast, with instruction for beginners or advanced sailors in sailing, boat handling, and navigation. Hiking and nature-watching opportunities. Can take slightly handicapped. Cost: $500/week.

**Angie Stringer or Trish or Larry Ulm, Sailboat Charters/Rentals Unlimited, 2046 Westlake Ave. N., Seattle, WA 98109; (206)283-4664.** Year-round sailboat charters offered from Anacortes or Seattle for minimum of 4 days. Twenty-five to 45-foot boats available, with or without skipper. Cost: $320 and up.

**San Juan Islands Cruising Center, P.O. Box 4164B, Squalicum Harbor, Bellingham, WA 98225; (206)671-2004.** Bareboat, or skippered, fully provisioned charters offered for sailing the San Juan Islands in summer, for as many days as desired. Boats range from 26 to 50 feet. Provisioning also available for bareboat charters if desired. Skippered charters have no fixed itinerary; guests decide destinations and activities. Cost: $200-225/day or $1,300-1,500/week for party of 2 to 4 persons for skippered charters; $400-1,800/week for bareboat charters.

**Doug Fischer, Wind Works Sailing School and Charters, 7001 Seaview Ave. N.W., Seattle, WA 98117; (206)784-9386.** Bareboat or skippered charters, instructional cruises, and custom excursions offered year-round, departing from Seattle or Anacortes. Other points of departure may be arranged. Sailing courses for novices up through advanced sailors offered. Certificate received upon completion of course allows 15 percent discount on Wind Works charters. Cost: $12 for 2 hours up to $450 for 5 days for skippered charters; $10 for 6 hours of classroom instruction; $55 for 8 hours or $99 for 16 hours of on-board instruction. (TA)

**Erni Bennett, Youth Adventure Inc., P.O. Box 23, Mercer Island, WA 98040; (206) 232-4024.** Nine-day instructional cruises aboard 101-foot schooner in Puget Sound and San Juan Islands for 14- to 18-year-olds, during weekends, vacation periods, and summer. Trainees serve as crew, standing watches, rotating galley duty, and sailing schooner when wind is favorable. Free time allows small-boat sailing, rowing, exploring. Cost: $225.

# California

**Oceanic Society Expeditions, Bldg. E, Fort Mason Center, San Francisco, CA 94123; (415)441-1106.** See Washington listing.

# SALTWATER CRUISING

One of the premier attractions of the Pacific Northwest is its saltwater sounds and bays, channels and straits. By chartering a cruise ship or by being a passenger on the regularly scheduled ferry runs up the coast, you can see the Northwest in one of the best possible ways at a cost small enough to be affordable for most families.

Puget Sound is the most accessible cruising ground in the region. From Washington's capital city of Olympia, the sound spreads out as it moves northward, past the residential islands of Vashon and Bainbridge near Seattle and up to Whidbey Island, the second longest island in the United States (following New York's Long Island). Between Vancouver Island and the American mainland are set the eight major and numerous minor islands that make up the San Juan chain. Some of the San Juans are inhabited year-round, some have only resort accommodations, some are privately owned, and some are home to no one except nesting bald eagles or other wild birds. All have beautiful wooded lands, unspoiled wilderness beaches, and the sunniest weather in western Washington, thanks to a local "sun shadow" climate condition. All in all, the San Juans are a perfect choice for nearby sailing or leisurely cruising.

There's an almost imperceptible change when you enter Canadian waters. It's not that the climate and terrain are that different—in fact, Vancouver Island itself dips well below the mainland boundary between the United States and Canada. But on the Inside Passage route from Tsawwassen, British Columbia, to Prince Rupert just south of Alaska's panhandle, the provincial ferries skirt one of the world's most spectacular coastlines. This is a land of fjords and pure streams that descend from the mountains above you and cascade directly into the salt waters of the passage. It also is the land of the Kwakiutl, the Haida, and the Tsimshian, native peoples whose imaginative art forms have become symbolic of the entire Northwest. They still live here, too, in fishing villages along the coast, watched over by giant totem poles. And it is a land whose cities and towns have grown up around the outposts established more than a century ago by the Hudson's Bay Company, thus providing it with a romantic modern history.

Cruising may demand less from a person than some other forms of travel, but the relative comfort of the accommodations on a private cruise ship or provincial ferry has its advantages. You can take more care with your photography and more pride in the finished results, you can explore some of the interesting small towns along your route, you can fish for salmon or bottom fish, and you sometimes can sight porpoises or killer whales as they ply the waters for food. Cruising these waters is an unforgettable—and uniquely Northwestern—experience.

# British Columbia

British Columbia Ferry Corporation, 818 Broughton St., Victoria, B.C., Canada V8V 1E4; (604)669-1211 or 386-3431. Inside Passage trip offered year-round. Cost: available upon request. (TA)

Arthur Tree, Heliousa Yacht Charters, 2551 Chelsea Pl., Victoria, B.C., Canada V8P 3E6; (604)477-9115. Skippered charter cruises of the sheltered coast of British Columbia on 38-foot motor cruiser between May and September. Guests encouraged to take part in yacht's handling and navigation; instruction in dinghy sailing provided if desired. Company provisions according to guests' specifications; guests cook for themselves and skipper. Cost: $840(Cdn.)/week for boat and skipper.

# Washington

Burton Nesset, Catalyst Charters, 515 S.

143rd St., Tacoma, WA 98444; (206) 537-7678. Six-day cruises to San Juan Islands, Hood Canal, and Victoria, between June 1 and September 1. Opportunity for hiking, fishing, beachcombing, and exploring. Group charters for shorter cruises also available. Cost: $360, includes all meals. (TA)

Explorer Cruise Lines, Suite 312, Park Place Bldg., Seattle, WA 98101; (800) 426-0600 or (206)624-5637. Four cruise itineraries ranging from 2 to 5 days offered on 41-stateroom ship. Cruises depart from Seattle and visit such places as LaConner, Rosario Resort, and Port Townsend in Washington, and Victoria and Princess Louisa Inlet in British Columbia. Cost: $585-1,110. (TA)

Ken McDonald, Viking Star Charters, 3629 Bagley N., Seattle, WA 98103; (206)634-2939. Three-day cruises from Seattle into the San Juan Islands, including a crab feast and visits to LaConner, Roche Harbor, and Rosario Resort, offered between May and October. Double-occupancy accommodations at the Islander Lopez on Lopez Island, which offers a golf course and heated pool. Cost: $199.

# SNOWSHOEING

A simple, ancient adaptation to winter weather, snowshoes may predate the migration of people to the New World, since examples of early snowshoes from North America and central Asia share the same basic design. That design has changed remarkably little over the centuries, though aluminum frames and nylon webbing have replaced the branch and bark materials of the traditional snowshoe. By distributing the body's weight over a surface area larger than the foot, snowshoes allow you to walk on snow without helplessly plunging into it.

In the Northwest, snowshoes are the means by which you can enjoy winter ventures into the Bugaboos of British Columbia, the Sierra Nevada of California, or the Cascades of Washington and Oregon for fishing, scenic hikes, or mountaineering expeditions. Many organized trips into these areas include instruction not only in snowshoeing but also in other aspects of winter travel, including shelter building, glacier travel, and ice fishing.

Snowshoes are not expensive, ranging from twenty dollars on up. They can be rented from many ski areas or mountain lodges and take but a few minutes to learn to use. While the waddling walk of the snowshoer may seem hilarious to an observer, those who try to do without them in snow soon cease to laugh.

# British Columbia

Loren Foss, Aerie Northwest, 4558 4th N.E., Seattle, WA 98105; (206)634-2849. Seven-day trip in Garibaldi Park in early April. Glaciers of the Fitzsimmons and Spearhead ranges are traversed, and as many of the easy 8,000-foot peaks en route as time will allow are climbed. Some climbing experience, including glacier training, winter- or snow-camping experience, and good physical condition required. Cost: $195.

Jack Eagleson, Eagle Recreations Inc., P.O. Box 1055, Lillooet, B.C., Canada V0K 1V0; (604)256-7300. Three-day snow-camping trips from Lillooet, in the heart of the Cariboos. In addition to snowshoeing, trips include cross-country skiing, ice fishing, and opportunity to enjoy outdoor Indian sauna. No experience or special equipment needed. Cost: $200/person; $180/person for parties of 4 or more.

Arnör Larson, Northern Lights Alpine Recreation, Box 399, Invermere, B.C., Canada V0A 1K0; (604)342-6042. Day-tours that include instruction, from mid-December to mid-March; trips of 1 or more weeks duration for mountain touring based at a remote log cabin, from early January to early April; or completely custom-tailored trips, from mid-November to late May. Groups are kept small to allow personal attention. Transportation to trailhead, food, and equipment not included. Cost: $20(Cdn.) for day-tours, $200/week for mountain cabin trips, $25-30/day for custom trips.

Jim or Myrna Boulding, Strathcona Park Lodge and Outdoor Education Centre, Box 2160, Campbell River, B.C., Canada V9W 5C9; Campbell River radio, Strathcona Lodge 59 7021. Overnight snowshoeing trips on weekends in January and February in the Elk River Valley. Mild winter weather allows for comfortable camping. Custom-tailored trips for 2 days to 2 weeks also offered, including accommodations, meals, instructor-guide, and equipment. Cost: $65(Cdn.) for overnight trips; $55/person/day for parties of less than 4, $45/person/day for parties of 4 or more for customized trips. (TA)

# Washington

Loren Foss, Aerie Northwest, 4558 4th N.E., Seattle, WA 98105; (206)634-2849. Winter-mountaineering course offered that includes instruction in snowshoeing. Course consists of 5 weekend field trips and 5 evening sessions. Prerequisites are a basic mountaineering course or equivalent training, some climbing and backpacking experience, and good physical condition. Cost: $270.

Bill or Peg Stark, Family Adventures, Inc., P.O. Box 312, Leavenworth, WA 98826; (509)548-7330. "Nomad camps," wilderness shelters for lodging and meals in the heart of the eastern Cascades, provide a base camp for snowshoers and cross-country skiers from mid-November to mid-May. More than 50 miles of excellent cross-country terrain. Three camps have dormitory and private lodging with thick foam mattresses, insulated floors, and wood stoves; full course, gourmet meals served. Cost: $20-88/day. (TA)

W. Gerald Lynch, Rainier Mountaineering, Inc., 201 St. Helens Ave., Tacoma, WA 98402; (206)627-6242. Snowshoeing instruction and rental equipment available in mid-winter. Cost: available upon request. (TA)

# Oregon

Ed Johann, Johann Mountain Guides, P.O.

Box 2334, Lincoln City, OR 97367; (503) 996-3232. Snowshoe trips offered featuring personable and personalized service. Guides are qualified mountaineers and instructors. Cost: $35/day. (TA)

# Idaho

Bob Liming, Alpine Wilderness Leadership School, 1801 Burrell Ave., Lewiston, ID 83501; (208)743-2478. Three- and 6-day field courses designed to teach skills necessary for living in comfort while traveling under winter conditions, using snowshoes as primary mode of travel. Cost: $40/day, includes food, equipment, and transportation to and from field site.

# California

Terry Halbert, Mountain People School, 157 Oak Spring Dr., San Anselmo, CA 94960; (415)457-3664. Overnight instructional trips in the Sierra Nevada to teach the basics of winter camping and snowshoeing. Classes are kept small to ensure individual attention and minimize impact on the land. Snowshoes and group equipment provided. Cost: $45.

# SOARING

Throughout history, an increasing array of devices has been invented to help fulfill man's dreams of being able to fly, and with the coming of the twentieth century these halting efforts have burst into fruition. The sport of soaring unites the grace of power-free flight with the benefits of technical advancement.

Though they were the direct precursors of today's complex airplanes, the first modern gliders had neither cockpits nor landing gear; present-day sailplanes, the most sophisticated of gliders, are masterpieces of aerodynamics and structure. They are easily controlled from within a closed cockpit and are capable of riding the winds for hours several miles above the earth's surface. Made of lightweight fiberglass or a fiberglass–balsa wood sandwich, the long wings and narrow fuselage of the sailplane permit glide ratios of better than forty to one—forty feet of forward motion for every foot of descent.

But the thing that sets sailplanes apart from other gliders is that they can soar—they can actually gain altitude by catching wind currents, much as birds do. They are launched by a tow from a small airplane or, sometimes, from a car on the ground. Once the proper altitude and speed have been reached, the pilot frees his craft by releasing a latch on the tow hook. Then the winds take over—winds that come up slopes, as at mountain ridges or coastal bluffs, or that rise in thermals over hot spots in flat land areas. A good pilot learns to recognize the terrain and cloud formations that signify "good" winds.

Soaring centers throughout the Northwest offer brief introductory flights in sailplanes. Usually, the passenger is permitted to sit in the front cockpit seat, which provides an unimpeded view of the Tetons of Idaho, San Francisco Bay, or other local landscapes. It even may be possible to maneuver the craft for awhile, pressing the foot pedals to control the rudders or swinging the universally hinged stick for elevator and aileron action. If you like even more excitement and your stomach is strong enough, you can probably persuade your pilot to make some aerobatic maneuvers, from loops and rolls to inverted flight and dizzying spins. Then it's time to turn back and make a gentle landing on the same airfield from which you took off an hour or so earlier.

# Idaho

**Klaus or Joyce Ansorge, Condor Sky Sailing, Box 1101, Hailey, ID 83333; (208) 788-3054 or 726-7547.** Scenic glider rides offered year-round over Sun Valley area. Pilots will demonstrate aerobatic maneuvers upon request. Courses offered leading to private glider pilot, commercial, or flight instruction certificates; "transition to glider" course for power pilots also available. Cost: $35 for 1 person, $55 for 2.

**Fred Reed, Red Baron Flying Service, Teton Peaks Airport, Driggs, ID 83422; (208)354-8131.** Year-round scenic glider rides over the Grand Tetons, offering excellent photographic opportunities. Passengers are allowed to handle controls if they wish after a demonstration by the pilot; pilot will also demonstrate aerobatic maneuvers upon request. Instruction offered leading to private glider pilot, commercial, or flight instruction certificates, as well as a "transition to glider" course for power pilots. Glider rentals also available to qualified pilots. Cost: $38 for ride.

# California

**Sky Sailing Airport, 44999 Christy St., Fremont, CA 94538; (415)656-9900.** Twenty- to 25-minute flights offered daily year-round over the San Francisco Bay area. Time can be reserved for large groups. Instruction also available. Cost: $23 for 1 person, $30 for 2.

# WILDERNESS SURVIVAL

You're out for a day of cross-country skiing, and a chance stumble over a ravine snaps a ski. As night approaches, you evaluate the little gear you have in your day pack, the several miles back to the road, and your chances of survival. Or you're on a week-long climbing expedition with friends, the weather has just taken a sudden, unseasonable change for the worse when one of your party loses his footing and breaks an ankle. What do you do?

As outdoor activities have increased in popularity, the frequency of accidents has also grown. Despite our more sophisticated supplies and equipment, it is just as important for today's outdoor enthusiast to learn wilderness survival skills as it was for yesterday's pioneer. Nature makes no special allowances for any of us.

Wilderness survival courses offer instruction in a wide variety of skills, suited to almost any emergency you might encounter. Orienteering and foraging for food may be emphasized in summer sessions while winter courses may include instruction in shelter building, and body warmth conservation. Guides are experienced, knowledgeable individuals, who teach not only the basic techniques of survival but also the more subtle aspects. For example, having route-finding skills may be your only chance to reach safety, but group dynamics can pull your party together or destroy it in an emergency situation.

No amount of instruction in a classroom or in a controlled situation can totally prepare someone for emergencies, which is why experiencing a close approximation to the real thing is an important feature of many survival courses. Solo overnight experiences, small group trips without guides, and simulated emergencies have been proven to be the best teaching methods, and several survival schools are built around these techniques. Naturally, participants in such programs are given the fullest possible training before taking the "final exam" of a solo or simulated emergency.

Many graduates of such programs speak of their own growth under the often severe conditions of training. These programs provide a means not only of learning a new set of skills but also of renewing, and in some cases creating, a sense of self-worth and self-sufficiency that can affect your everyday life.

structors to test teamwork and knowledge of physical environment. Courses also include solo time—each student alone with minimal provisions—and a marathon event. Cost: $465-750.

**Jim or Myrna Boulding, Strathcona Park Lodge and Outdoor Education Centre, Box 2160, Campbell River, B.C., Canada V9W 5C9; Campbell River radio, Strathcona Lodge 59 7021.** Fast-paced, 6-day wilderness survival course with instruction in fire lighting, shelter building, edible and useful plants, basic first aid, survival psychology, and wild animal behavior. Overnight camp provides focus for much of the learning. Course offered in August. Cost: $250(Cdn.). (TA)

# Washington

**Loren Foss, Aerie Northwest, 4558 4th N.E., Seattle, WA 98105; (206)634-2349.** Courses in alpine travel and mountaineering with goal of equipping students for independent wilderness experiences. Courses consist of several weekend trips and evening sessions and are offered from January through June. Cost: $170-290.

**Dunham Gooding, North Cascades Alpine School, 1212 24th St. W., Bellingham, WA 98225; (206)671-1505.** Six-day alpine mountaineering courses intended to serve as intensive introduction to all aspects of off-trail alpine travel, including rock-, snow-, and ice-climbing skills, minimum-impact travel and camping, survival techniques, and orienteering. Courses offered June through September. Cost: $220.

**Northwest Outward Bound School, 0110 S.W. Bancroft, Portland, OR 97201; (503) 243-2993.** Eight-, 14-, and 24-day courses designed to bring about personal and social growth in participants through intensive wilderness experience. Year-round courses involve backcountry travel,

# British Columbia

Canadian Outward Bound Mountain School, 1616 W. 77th Ave., Vancouver, B.C., Canada V6J 1S5; (604)733-9104. Three- to 4-week courses in basic wilderness skills, designed to bring about personal and social growth in participants. Instructors guide early trips; students go on final expedition without in-

mountaineering, and physical conditioning activities, and include instruction in campcraft, route finding, first aid, and rock climbing. Customized courses available for groups and organizations. Cost: $400 for 8-day courses, $600 for 14-day courses, $750 for 24-day courses.

# Oregon

**Northwest Outward Bound School, 0110 S.W. Bancroft, Portland, OR 97201; (503) 243-1993.** See Washington listing.

# Idaho

**Bob Liming, Alpine Wilderness Leadership School, 1801 Burrell Ave., Lewiston, ID 93501; (208)743-2478.** Year-round courses in wilderness skills including mountaineering, backpacking, outdoor behavior, survival, and nature appreciation. After 2-day orientation at base camp, courses are taught in the field, in the Clearwater and Nez Perce national forests. Cost: $35/day.

**Northwest Outward Bound School, 0110 S.W. Bancroft, Portland, OR 97201; (503) 243-1993.** See Washington listing.

# California

**Terry Halbert, Mountain People School, 157 Oak Spring Dr., San Anselmo, CA 94960; (415)457-3664.** One- and 2-week backpacking courses including instruction in campcraft, cooking, map reading and navigation, survival, first aid, and rock climbing. Participants meet in San Rafael, courses are conducted in the Sierra Nevada. Classes are kept small to ensure individual attention and minimize impact on the land. Cost: $150 for 1-week courses, $280 for 2-week courses.

**Mark Ewing, Squaw Valley Nordic Center, P.O. Box 2499, Olympic Valley, CA 95730; (916)583-4284.** One-day survival clinics designed for the backcountry tourer who would like to increase winter survival skills. Courses are taught in the field and include instruction in clothing and equipment, hypothermia, emergency wilderness first aid, shelter building, and topographic map interpretation. Cost: $15.

**Yosemite Mountaineering School and Guide Service, Yosemite National Park, CA 95389; (209)372-4611 ext. 244.** Ski-touring survival courses including how to build a no-tool shelter, conserving energy and body heat, building fires, first aid, etc.; alpine survival courses concentrating on food and warmth; and alpine survival courses emphasizing wilderness hazards and navigation. All are 1-day courses meeting on weekends. Alpine survival is offered in spring and summer, ski-touring survival in winter. Cost: $12 for ski-touring survival courses; $16 for alpine survival courses.

# WINDSURFING

Though the sport is only ten years old, windsurfing already has proven its success by becoming a life-style for many outdoor enthusiasts. Using an inspired combination of sailing and surfing techniques, the windsurfer steers his board by hanging onto the wishbone-shaped boom and directs it to skim across the waters of lakes, sheltered shorelines, and even open seas.

As might be expected, such an activity is most popular in Hawaii and California, longtime centers for both parent sports. But in the Northwest an increasing number of people are finding that the moderate spring and summer weather here is perfect for windsurfing. There may not be as many sunny days as in the south, but there certainly are enough to make possible a steady string of windsurfing events from March to October. Lightweight wet suits, too, can extend the limits of time a person can enjoyably spend in the water on any given day, and the weeks of the year during which the sport can be savored.

It takes no special skills to learn windsurfing—only agility and coordination. The polyurethane board is twelve feet long, the mast fourteen feet high, and the nylon sail fifty-six square feet in area. The entire setup, including board and teak or aluminum mast and boom, weighs about sixty-five pounds and requires very little rigging.

Once you learn the basic techniques of windsurfing, usually teachable in four or five hours, you can perform many maneuvers, from backward sailing to riding the rail to wave jumping. The limits of windsurfing, as in so many adventure sports, are set by your imagination as much as by your skills. To glide silently across clear water with the sun at your back and the wind in your face: what better way to enjoy the blessings of summer?

# British Columbia

Gordon Greer Ltd., 377 Davis St., Comox, B.C., Canada V9N 4N3; (604)339-4914. Five-day windsurfing vacation, including 2-day course and 3 half-day practice sessions, in area suited to both beginners and experts. Can begin any day from April 12 to September 30. All equipment provided. Cost: $99.

# Washington

Doug Baker, White Water Sports, Inc., 307 N.E. 71st, Seattle, WA 98115; (206)523-5150. Windsurfing weekend in summer at Lake Chelan, with instruction, equipment, and round-trip transportation from Seattle provided. Instruction and rental equipment also available in Seattle. Cost: $90 for weekend at Lake Chelan; $50 for two 2-hour lessons, including equipment, in Seattle.

# PHOTO CREDITS

**Numerals indicate pages on which photos appear.**

# OTHER BOOKS FROM PACIFIC SEARCH PRESS

*Spinning and Weaving with Wool*
    by Paula Simmons
*Starchild & Holahan's Seafood Cookbook*
    by Adam Starchild and James
    Holahan
*Two Crows Came* by Jonni Dolan
*The Whole Grain Bake Book*
    by Gail L. Worstman
*Why Wild Edibles? The Joys of Finding,*
    *Fixing, and Tasting*
    by Russ Mohney
*Wild Mushroom Recipes* by Puget
    Sound Mycological Society
*Wild Shrubs: Finding and Growing*
    *Your Own* by Joy Spurr
*The Zucchini Cookbook*
    by Paula Simmons